Kierkegaard: A Very Short Introduction

'Marvellously lucid and readable book.'
E. Pivcevic, University of Bristol

'Lucid sketch for the beginner of the thinking of the man who initially
discarded theology for philosophy and literature, and subsequently
influenced theology more.'
Theological Book Review

Very Short Introductions available now:

Patrick Gardiner

KIERKEGAARD

A Very Short Introduction

OXFORD
UNIVERSITY PRESS

OXFORD
UNIVERSITY PRESS

Great Clarendon Street, Oxford OX2 6DP

Oxford University Press is a department of the University of Oxford.
It furthers the University's objective of excellence in research, scholarship,
and education by publishing worldwide in

Oxford New York

Auckland Bangkok Buenos Aires Cape Town Chennai
Dar es Salaam Delhi Hong Kong Istanbul Karachi Kolkata
Kuala Lumpur Madrid Melbourne Mexico City Mumbai Nairobi
São Paulo Shanghai Taipei Tokyo Toronto

Oxford is a registered trade mark of Oxford University Press
in the UK and in certain other countries

Published in the United States
by Oxford University Press Inc., New York

© Patrick Gardiner 1988

The moral rights of the author have been asserted
Database right Oxford University Press (maker)

First published as an Oxford University Press paperback 1988
First published as a Very Short Introduction 2002

British Library Cataloguing in Publication Data

Data available

Library of Congress Cataloging in Publication Data

Data available

ISBN 978-0-19-280256-9

19 20 18

Typeset by RefineCatch Ltd, Bungay, Suffolk
Printed in Great Britain by
Ashford Colour Press Ltd, Gosport, Hampshire

Contents

Preface

The range and diversity of Kierkegaard's literary production do not make the task of providing a short introduction to his thought an easy one. Rather than attempting to cover all its different aspects, I have felt it better to focus attention chiefly upon those that were most closely related to the intellectual and cultural preoccupations of the period to which he belonged. Amongst other things I have sought to trace the considerations that led him to develop his own distinctive positions concerning the status of ethics and religion, while at the same time indicating some of the ways in which he exercised an important, if delayed, influence upon the subsequent history of ideas. This limitation of scope has meant, however, omitting from discussion various of his many publications, including ones where he addressed himself most directly to the nature of the religious life as he believed that it should be understood.

In part of chapter 4 I have drawn upon certain material previously published in a lecture which I delivered to the British Academy several years ago: it appears here in a considerably revised and altered form.

Abbreviations

The following abbreviations are used in references to Kierkegaard's works:

CA   *The Concept of Anxiety*, tr. R. Thomte and A. B. Anderson (Princeton University Press, 1980)

CUP   *Concluding Unscientific Postscript*, tr. D. F. Swenson and W. Lowrie (Princeton University Press, 1941)

EO   *Either/Or*, 2 vols., tr. D. F. and L. M. Swenson and W. Lowrie (Princeton University Press, 1959)

FT   *Fear and Trembling* and *Repetition*, tr. H. V. and E. H. Hong (Princeton University Press, 1983)

J   *The Journals of Soren Kierkegaard*, tr. A. Dru (Oxford University Press, 1938)

PA   *The Present Age*, tr. A. Dru (Fontana Library, 1962)

PF   *Philosophical Fragments*, tr. D. F. Swenson, rev. H. V. Hong (Princeton University Press, 1962)

PV   *The Point of View of my Work as an Author*, tr. W. Lowrie (Harper and Row, 1962)

SD   *The Sickness unto Death*, tr. H. V. and E. H. Hong (Princeton University Press, 1980)

SLW   *Stages on Life's Way*, tr. W. Lowrie (Schocken Books, 1967)

List of illustrations

Chapter 1
Life and character

Kierkegaard on more than one occasion likened genius to a thunderstorm that comes up against the wind. Whether or not he had himself partly in mind when making the comparison, it seems in retrospect to have been an apt one so far as his own intellectual career was concerned. Like Marx and Nietzsche, he emerges as one of the outstanding iconoclasts and rebels of 19th-century thought, writers whose works were composed in conscious opposition to the prevailing assumptions and conventions of their age and whose crucial contentions only achieved widespread recognition after they were dead.

In Kierkegaard's case recognition was particularly slow in coming. He wrote in Danish, and to his Danish contemporaries he was – in his own eyes at least – a 'superfluous' figure; either they did not read what he wrote or else, if they did, they misunderstood its underlying import. Even when, not very long after his death in 1855, German translations began to appear, they made little initial impact, although they were to become increasingly influential in Central Europe during and immediately after the First World War. It was, however, largely through its association with existentialism, which emerged as a well-publicized philosophical movement in the 1930s and 1940s, that his name can first be said to have acquired the kind of international prominence it indisputably enjoys today. As a thinker he may be regarded as awkward, controversial, difficult to classify; but he is certainly not ignored.

Such posthumous fame would in fact have caused Kierkegaard no surprise. He himself confidently predicted it, foreseeing a time when his books would be the subject of serious study and when he would be applauded for the novelty and depth of the insights they contained. Whether, on the other hand, it would have afforded him undiluted satisfaction is a different matter. When he referred to the prospect he treated it as an occasion, not for self-congratulation, but for sardonic comment. For the persons whose approbation he anticipated were those he labelled 'professors'; in other words, future members of the selfsame academic institutions which during his lifetime were the target of some of his sharpest criticism. Admittedly his opinions on this score, like the pronounced antipathy he came to feel towards the Church, were voiced most stridently towards the end of his career. None the less, his hostility to the academic establishment was continuous with an earlier and deep-rooted suspicion of something that he believed to be endemic to the intellectual climate of his period. This was its preoccupation with what he called the 'illusions of objectivity', exhibiting itself, on the one hand, in a tendency to smother the vital core of subjective experience beneath layers of historical commentary and pseudo-scientific generalization and, on the other, in a proneness to discuss ideas from an abstract theoretical viewpoint that took no account of their significance for the particular outlooks and commitments of flesh-and-blood human beings. All Kierkegaard's writings, in one way or another, bore witness to the necessity of affirming the integrity of the individual in the face of such trends, and the same can be said to have been true of his life. His work and his personal existence were indeed inseparably intertwined, the connections between the two being faithfully recorded in the copious journals which he kept from the age of 21 onwards and which throw a vivid light upon the labyrinthine recesses of his strange and complex disposition.

Søren Aabye Kierkegaard was born in Copenhagen on 5 May 1813. He was the seventh child of Michael Pedersen Kierkegaard, a retired hosier who had been released from serfdom in his youth and who had since become relatively wealthy, partly through his own efforts but also as a result of inheriting a considerable fortune from an uncle. Kierkegaard's mother, whom his father had married after the early death of his first wife, had been the latter's maid; she was illiterate and appears to have played a somewhat shadowy part in her son's upbringing. His father, by contrast, was a dominant influence. Self-educated and shrewd in business, he was at the same time a devout member of the Lutheran Church with a strong belief in duty and self-discipline. Kierkegaard was later to recall the 'absolute obedience' that was demanded of him as a child, but it was not this that made the greatest impression upon him. More potent, at any rate in its subsequent effects, was the atmosphere of gloom and religious guilt that emanated from a parent who believed that both he and his

1. Portrait of Kierkegaard. Unknown artist.

family lay under a mysterious curse and who, notwithstanding his worldly success, lived in constant expectation of divine retribution. Thus, in a retrospective entry in his journals, his son could speak of 'the dark background which, from the very earliest time, was part of my life' and recollect the 'dread with which my father filled my soul, his own frightful melancholy, and all the things in this connection which I do not even note down' (J 273).

Although he was never at any stage one to underestimate the personal disabilities and difficulties that beset him, there is a poignancy about such remarks which makes it understandable that Kierkegaard should have stigmatized the manner in which he had been brought up as 'insane'. Even so, his feelings towards the man who evoked them were ambivalent: he was fascinated by his father's vivid if morbid imagination, appears to have been impressed by his intellect and powers of argument, and always remained bound to his memory by some profound emotional affinity that involved a strange mixture of love and fear.

If his life at home was conducted in what one of his childhood companions portrayed as a mystical twilight of 'strictness and eccentricity', Kierkegaard's career at the private school he attended does not seem to have afforded him much in the way of relief. As a boy he was physically weak and maladroit, and at the same time acutely self-conscious about what he felt to be his unprepossessing appearance; in consequence, he played no part in games and tended to be a natural prey to bullies. He was, however, far from being defenceless in other respects. He quickly became aware of his superior intelligence, admitting later that this provided him with an effective weapon by which to protect himself against those who threatened him. He had a sharp and wounding tongue, was perceptive in spotting the vulnerable points of others, and from all accounts was an adept and provocative tease, capable of reducing members of his class to tears. As a result, he put a distance between himself and those around him, a lonely,

2. Nytorv (New Square), Copenhagen, in 1865. The town where Kierkegaard was born.

introverted figure who inspired apprehension rather than affection. The picture painted by his contemporaries at school may not be an altogether attractive one. Nevertheless, it is not without intimations of the angular independence of mind and the talent for ridicule that were to be amongst his most immediately striking characteristics as an adult. In 1830, at the age of 17, Kierkegaard enrolled as a student at the University of Copenhagen. Initially things went well enough. During his first year he covered preliminary courses in a wide range of subjects; they included Greek and Latin, history, mathematics, physics, and philosophy, and he passed all the relevant examinations with distinction. He then began reading for a degree in theology, following in the footsteps of his academically gifted but rather priggish elder brother, Peter; the latter had already completed the course in less than the usual time and was now working for a doctorate in Germany. In Søren's case, however, matters were not to proceed so smoothly. His progress towards the degree gradually lost momentum and by 1835 he was writing to a friend that taking the course was an occupation that did not in the least interest him; he 'preferred a free and perhaps . . . a somewhat indefinite study to the *table d'hôte* where one knows in advance the guests and the menu for each day of the week' (J 9). This description of his attitude in fact reflected the mode of life he was pursuing at the time, one that seems to have been adopted in deliberate defiance of the austere ideals and cheese-paring precepts to which his family environment had accustomed him. He spent money freely on clothes and drink, running up debts which he relied on his father to pay; he also attended a round of parties, frequented cafés and restaurants, and was continually to be seen at the theatre and opera where, in his own words, he appeared as 'a man in modern dress, glasses on his nose and a cigar in his mouth'.

Kierkegaard once said of himself that he was a two-faced Janus – 'with the one face I laugh, with the other I weep (J 47). However much he may have appeared to have been enjoying himself during his protracted career as a student, what he wrote in his journals throughout this period reveals that he was profoundly dissatisfied with the emptiness of his existence and with his inability to find some centre or focus for his life. On the one hand, he complains of the futility of seeking pleasures which invariably left in their wake feelings of ennui and malaise; on the other, he expresses impatience with learning in so far as this is regarded as a purely dispassionate pursuit of knowledge and understanding – 'what good would it do me if truth stood before me, cold and naked, not caring whether I recognized her or not?' (J 15). Instead, he speaks of the need to discover an 'idea' or 'life-view' with which he can unreservedly identify himself and casts an envious eye upon those 'great men' who, irrespective of the cost, have whole-heartedly committed themselves to the realization of projects which appeared to them to be supremely worthwhile; at one point, indeed, he seems even to have found the conception of a single-minded master criminal an appealing one. It is

Jannskopf (römischer As).

3. Kierkegaard likened himself to Janus, the two-faced god, saying 'with the one face I laugh, with the other I weep.'

true that he was reading intensively, philosophy and literature taking the place of the theology he had discarded and providing a rich field for the exercise of his critical and imaginative powers. In doing so, however, he felt that he was essentially occupying the role of a spectator rather than of an agent, perpetually reliving the experiences and thoughts of others while failing to achieve anything on his own account. Thus he described himself as existing in the 'subjunctive' as opposed to the 'indicative' mood and despairingly compared his position to that of a chess piece which could not be moved.

This period of Kierkegaard's life, in which an outward display of gaiety and insouciance can be said to have masked a deep sense of personal inadequacy and confusion, lasted until the sudden death of his father in 1838. In view of the peculiarly close yet uneasy relationship which had subsisted between the two, it was to be expected that the event would produce a powerful emotional impact. What was perhaps less predictable was the form it took. Out of a family of seven children only two had survived, and Kierkegaard appears to have assumed that his father was destined to outlive himself and his brother as well. When this did not happen he interpreted his father's death as involving some sort of 'sacrifice' which had been made on his behalf so that 'if possible I might turn into something' (J 62). Hence, notwithstanding a comfortable inheritance that removed any practical incentive for acquiring the degree, he now saw himself as under an obligation to fulfil his parent's wish that he should complete his university course and he at once started seriously to prepare himself for the examination. The consequence was that within two years his outlook and prospects seemed to have undergone a radical transformation. Shortly after his father died he published his first book, a critical study of Hans Andersen's limitations as a novelist which he entitled *From the Papers of One Still Living*. In July 1840 he was at long last awarded his degree in theology. By September of the same year he had announced his engagement to the daughter of Terkel Olsen, a highly placed and well-connected civil servant, and in the following November he both embarked on a training course at a pastoral seminary and began work on a master's thesis at the university. All in all, and with his days as a dilettante and a *flâneur* far behind him, he looked set upon pursuing a professional career as a responsible married man.

Nevertheless, appearances were once again deceptive. The memory of his engagement to Regine Olsen was certainly to play a central part in Kierkegaard's subsequent development, both as a person and as a writer: it was something to which he obsessively returned in numerous journal entries, and disguised references to it constantly recur at different stages of his literary production. Going by his later account of what happened, however, he was from the start divided in his own mind about the idea of marriage and an aura of unreality – on his side at least – seems to have surrounded the relationship at the time. On the surface he may have given the impression that all was well, conscientiously doing everything that might have been expected from one in his position. Even so; he maintained that he regretted making the proposal the day after it was accepted and as the months passed his doubts and anxieties were to become increasingly acute, though always apparently carefully concealed. Almost a year passed before he took the step of returning the ring, asking Regine to forget the man who sent it and to forgive him as being one who was not capable of making a girl happy. After a further period during which she made strenuous efforts to win him back, he decided to repel her with a show of careless indifference in the belief that, as he later put it, this was the only thing he could do to 'push her into marrying someone else'.

Whatever the outside world might think of his behaviour – and he did nothing at the time to present it in a light favourable to himself – Kierkegaard claimed in retrospect that the breaking off of the engagement was a self-inflicted wound which caused him intense inward suffering. Nor can it really be doubted that this was so. As he described the situation, he found himself compelled to take an agonizing decision in which his own feelings were profoundly involved;

the conviction that the choice he made was the right one in no way alleviated the anguish it entailed. It must be admitted, all the same, that he was somewhat evasive about the nature of the reasons that lay behind it; at times he spoke of a consciousness of personal inadequacy deriving from his 'melancholy', at others of a fundamental incompatibility of temperament, and at others again of his own calling as an 'exceptional' individual which ultimately ruled out the possibility of his ever entering into so demanding a relationship with someone else. But, whatever the truth of the matter, there can at least be no question that the separation from Regine Olsen represented a crucial turning point in his life. Although his commitment to Christianity itself was by now fixed and unalterable, the prospect of following his brother and taking up a career in the Church was no longer viewed by him as a serious option. Instead he retired into private existence as a bachelor, using the considerable income that had accrued to him from his father's estate as a basis upon which to devote himself exclusively to writing. 'To produce', he remarked on a later occasion, 'was my life.'

4. Kierkegaard's house, 'Achtwegehaus'.

Literary production was, indeed, already under way. It is perhaps an index of Kierkegaard's ambivalent state of mind during the period of his ill-fated engagement that the emotional problems it posed can in no sense be said to have distracted him from his work. On the contrary, if anything they appear to have had the reverse effect and to have initiated a remarkable burst of activity whose immediate consequence was the completion of his master's dissertation – *On the Concept of Irony with Particular Reference to Socrates* – less than a year after he began it. Its convoluted style seems to have worried his examiners, one of whom complained of its prolixity and artificiality, and they may also have been surprised by the novelty of his approach. In a manner that foreshadowed many of his subsequent writings he already showed himself – at least by implication – to be critical of certain aspects of the widely respected Hegelian philosophy, and he also drew freely if obliquely upon his personal experience when he characterized the romantic ironist as being 'a stranger and an alien' to the world, perpetually living at one remove from both others and himself. None the less, and whatever reservations may have been felt at the time, the thesis was passed by the university faculty.

Later in the same year (1841) Kierkegaard left Copenhagen for Berlin. His professed object in doing so was to attend a course of lectures given by Schelling, a German philosopher who had been closely associated with Hegel in his youth but who had afterwards turned against him and was now well known for his uncompromising opposition to the latter's ideas. Kierkegaard was at first favourably struck by what he heard, sympathizing with Schelling's contention that, in attempting to reduce the realm of concrete actuality to the unfolding of general concepts or categories, Hegel had failed to grasp the crucial distinction between essence and existence. As the lectures progressed from negative criticism to positive speculation, however, he became increasingly exasperated by Schelling's woolly pretentiousness and by the 'impotence' of his metaphysical doctrines; in any case, he was by this time fully engaged upon an undertaking of his own. 'Schelling drivels on quite intolerably', he wrote in a letter to his brother in the following February, going on to say that he had decided to return to Copenhagen to finish 'a little work I have in hand' (J 104). The work in question was to be entitled *Either/Or* and constituted the first of a series of books on philosophical, literary, and psychological themes which he wrote in rapid succession during the next few years. *Either/Or* itself, far from being 'little', was published in two substantial volumes at the beginning of 1843; eight months later *Repetition* and *Fear and Trembling* appeared, to be followed by *Philosophical Fragments* and *The Concept of Anxiety* (both in June 1844), *Stages on Life's Way* (1845), and *Concluding Unscientific Postscript* (1846). Nor did these works, all of which were presented to the public under a variety of pseudonyms, exhaust Kierkegaard's output during the period: in addition, he published 18 *Edifying Discourses* which appeared under his own name and which differed from the pseudonymous writings in being of an expressly religious character. Such productivity was impressive by any standards, but it had been achieved at a considerable cost to himself; mentally exhausted after almost half a decade when he had worked 'like a clerk in his office, perhaps without a single day's break', it is hardly surprising that on the completion of his *Postscript* he considered abandoning authorship and retiring to a living in the country. Yet whatever plans he may have entertained in this connection were interrupted by an event that was to leave an indelible imprint on his mind.

In December 1845 a collection of literary essays was published which included a critical discussion of Kierkegaard's *Stages on Life's Way*. Personal in tone and censorious by implication of his treatment of Regine Olsen, it was written by P. L. Møller, a man with whom he had been acquainted in his student years and who now harboured the ambition of succeeding to a university professorship. Kierkegaard had a poor opinion of Møller's own moral character; he was aware, too, that Møller secretly contributed to *The Corsair*, a satirical weekly which made a practice of holding up to ridicule people prominent in Copenhagen society but which had so far treated Kierkegaard himself with respect.

Incensed by the article and armed with this knowledge, he responded to its criticisms by bitterly attacking Møller in a piece that disclosed the latter's covert association with disreputable journalism; at the same time he issued what amounted to a challenge to *The Corsair* to include him amongst its victims, suggesting that it was more discreditable to be honoured by such a paper than to be insulted by it. Inasmuch as Møller's own reputation and prospects had been severely damaged, Kierkegaard's invective was effective; but it also had the less welcome consequence of rebounding against himself. The editor of *The Corsair* took up the challenge thrown down to him and for week after week Kierkegaard was pilloried, both verbally and pictorially, in a fashion that spared neither his physical appearance nor his habits. The public humiliation he suffered as a result was deeply wounding, as the following extract from his journals makes clear:

> Even the butcher's boy almost thinks himself justified in being offensive to me at the behest of *The Corsair*. Undergraduates grin and giggle and are delighted that someone prominent should be trodden down; the dons are envious and secretly sympathize with the attack, help to spread it abroad, adding of course that it is a crying shame. The least thing I do, even if I simply pay a visit, is lyingly distorted and repeated everywhere; if *The Corsair* gets to know of it then it is printed and is read by the whole population.

(J 161)

He went on to complain that even those whose company he enjoyed found it embarrassing or irritating to be with him, for fear that the mockery should rub off on to them – 'in the end the only thing will be to withdraw and only go about with those I dislike, for it is really a shame to go about with the others.'

The suggestion that acquaintances from whom he might have expected support were deserting him may or may not have been justified, but it is certainly indicative of the almost paranoiac feeling of isolation that he suffered at this moment of his life. As time went on, however, Kierkegaard began to look at his situation, and the action that had given rise to it, in a more positive light. Not only had he made a stand against the threat posed by a certain kind of prying journalism; he had been prepared to undergo the consequences of doing so in his own person. Furthermore, he had been made aware at first hand of the cowardice with which people were ready to submit to majority opinion and the lack of respect for the integrity of the individual that was a corollary of this. With such experiences behind him, he finally discarded his previous notion of retiring to a country parish and became convinced instead that current 'literary, social and political conditions' required the services of an 'extraordinarius' who was ready to speak out in the name of the truth. The truth in question was that of Christianity and he regarded his own intellectual gifts and cast of mind as properly fitting him for the task. It was, indeed, with the sense of one endowed with a providential mission that he decided to remain faithful to his literary vocation, speaking of the need he felt once more to 'steer into the open sea, living in grace and out of grace, entirely in the power of God' (J 192).

Hence, although the traumatic incidents of 1846 continued to reverberate in his memory, Kierkegaard's life resumed the outwardly uneventful but inwardly strenuous course it had followed before. His mode of conducting it was certainly not lacking in material compensations, and he drew heavily on his substantial inheritance in order to ensure that he worked in congenial conditions: thus he regularly arranged for elaborate meals to be brought to his elegantly furnished apartment, he indulged his taste for good wine, and in the summer he continued his practice of hiring carriages to take him for drives in the country. While freely admitting to his extravagance, he insisted that his writing depended upon his living in a congenial style; nevertheless, the message he now employed it to convey was far from being a comfortable one. Convinced that contemporary society was generally riddled with complacency, hypocrisy, and self-deception and that these were particularly manifest in the sphere of religious thought and observance, he set out to shock people into a correct awareness of their situation. Such works as *A Literary Review* (1846), *Edifying Discourses in Various Spirits* and *Works of Love* (1847), and *Christian Discourses* (1848) prepared the way for two major books – both, unlike their immediate predecessors, published under a pseudonym – whereby he sought to bring his readers to a proper understanding of what was involved: *The Sickness unto Death* (1849), a probing study in spiritual pathology that was in some ways continuous with his earlier *Concept of Anxiety*, and *Training in Christianity* (1850), in which a trenchant contrast was drawn between the outlook the Christian faith actually demands of a believer and the facile or worldly surrogates that are widely disseminated in its name. And these productions in their turn can be seen as foreshadowing a step whose repercussions formed the climax of Kierkegaard's career.

During the early 1850s he in fact published a relatively small amount; yet this was to prove to be no more than an interlude before his hostility to prevalent trends took a more openly subversive direction, focusing in the first instance upon the reputation of a respected Church dignitary. In 1854 Bishop Mynster, the Danish primate, died and was succeeded in the office by Hans Martensen, a theologian who had previously been one of Kierkegaard's university tutors. In his funeral oration Martensen referred to Mynster as 'a witness to the truth', a phrase which struck his former pupil as being peculiarly inept; although Mynster had been a personal friend of his father, Kierkegaard himself had increasingly come to regard him as exemplifying the self-satisfied and undemanding approach to Christianity which he had denounced in his own work. Accordingly, in December of the same year he wrote an article pouring scorn on what Martensen had said, subsequently going on to widen his target to include everything that official Christianity – 'Christendom' – stood for and casting cynical aspersions upon the underlying motivation of its proponents and representatives. At the heart of his campaign, initially conducted in the public press and later through the medium of a broadsheet called 'The Instant', which was printed at his own expense, lay the contention that the Church had become an essentially secular institution, hand in glove with the State and ruled by a bureaucracy whose prime concern was to further the material interests of its members. This had taken place behind a screen of hypocritical verbiage that concealed the true aims of its activities and where the terms used had to be interpreted in an inverted sense if their real import was to be discovered. Preaching the Word in poverty, for example, should be understood to mean pursuing a profitable career, and the renunciation of earthly goods the acquisition of such goods; the situation was comparable to one in which a man regularly employed the word 'farewell' in order to indicate that he had arrived – 'how could it occur to anyone on hearing the word "farewell" that a person is arriving?' Thus Kierkegaard implied that a gigantic confidence trick was being played upon those whom the Church professed to serve, and he finally called on his readers to withdraw altogether from 'official worship' if they wished to avoid participating in practices that amounted to making a fool of God.

Kierkegaard's single-handed attack on the clerical establishment was pursued with a polemical force and a sarcastic venom that have reminded some recent commentators of the zest with which his contemporary, Karl Marx, sought to unmask the ideological pretensions of 19th-century capitalist society. It undoubtedly occasioned anger, even alarm, in some quarters, and representations were made demanding action against what was regarded as disruptive agitation. But his violent foray into the field of public controversy turned out to be short-lived. Early in October 1855 he collapsed in the street, dying in hospital a few weeks later. He was accorded a funeral service in Copenhagen Cathedral, and in an address to the large congregation his brother mingled appreciation for his work with regret for the confused judgement he had displayed during the last phase of his life. Had Kierkegaard known of them in advance, the irony of these proceedings would hardly have escaped him.

Chapter 2
Philosophical background

Whatever their differences on other counts, Kierkegaard's numerous commentators have tended to agree that he was not a philosopher in any customary or traditional sense of the term. Thus in a general way it has been maintained that there is a striking lack of affinity between the overall style and direction of his own thinking and the typical methods and objectives of philosophical enquiry which had taken shape during the two hundred years or so before he wrote. Readers who come to his work in the expectation of being confronted by clear lines of argument, proceeding from carefully formulated premises and issuing in determinate conclusions, will often be disappointed; in this respect his characteristic modes of presenting his ideas stand in sharp contrast, not only to the rigorous procedures adopted by systematic theorists like Descartes and Spinoza, but also to the more informal patterns of demonstration favoured by such empirically minded writers as Locke and Berkeley. Nor, again, was he centrally concerned with topics of the kind that formed the focus of philosophical attention in the 17th and 18th centuries; questions concerning the fundamental structure of the universe or the nature and scope of our knowledge of reality were not amongst those that he principally sought to pursue. And it may further be argued that the theoretical ambitions which had largely inspired his great predecessors – ambitions profoundly influenced by the sweeping advances that had been achieved in the physical sciences – were in any case ones to which he was, both by temperament and by conviction, deeply averse. The very conception of the 'speculative' thinker, set apart from the contingencies of everyday living and coolly contemplating existence from a privileged vantage-point, was apt to arouse his suspicion, even antipathy; amongst other things, he was prone to treat it as involving a bland indifference to what mattered to people as individuals whose real interests found no recognition at the hands of 'systematists and objective philosophers'. In the light of all this it is perhaps not surprising that some critics have portrayed him as being an extreme representative of the Romantic revolt against the ideals of the European Enlightenment, while in the eyes of others he has been viewed as an anti-philosopher rather than a philosopher, not merely out of sympathy with the aims of dispassionate enquiry but actively intent upon undermining the assumptions of those who pursued it.

Consideration of some of these claims must be left until later. But in any event it would be quite mistaken to suppose that Kierkegaard's ideas and intentions can be understood without appreciating their connections with matters that were the subject of widespread controversy amongst philosophers at the time at which he wrote. It may be true that in a general way his leading interests were not continuous with those that had dominated the mainstream of previous philosophical discussion; none the less, the latter had brought in its wake a number of issues which were indisputably central to his own deepest preoccupations. These issues concerned both the ethical and the religious dimensions of human experience, and they had emerged in a manner that raised fundamental questions about the status and justification of each. Thus, if from one standpoint Kierkegaard's writings may seem to reflect concerns deriving from his personal life and character, from another they can be regarded as responses to what he himself clearly conceived to be the challenge presented by pervasive tendencies in the moral and religious thinking of his age.

Kant and Hume

What sort of challenge was involved and how had it arisen? The most
convenient starting point is to be found in certain ideas developed
towards the close of the 18th century by Immanuel Kant (1724–1804).
Whatever may be said about Kierkegaard's approach, Kant's own
philosophy was undeniably orientated towards problems that lay at the
heart of the philosophical enterprise as this was understood in his day.
He himself never wavered in the belief that it was necessary to come to
terms with the achievements of natural science in the exploration of the
physical world; more specifically, he never questioned the significance
of the Newtonian world-picture or sought to minimize the importance
of its implications for the future of systematic enquiry. At the same
time, however, he was acutely aware of the disputes that had arisen at a
philosophical level as to how much such enquiry could properly be said
to encompass. Were empirical methods of the type employed by
natural scientists the only ones available to us, or was it possible – as
some theorists had contended – to acquire a superior insight into reality
which was not subject to empirical constraints and which could be
attained solely on the basis of ideas and principles whose validity was
transparent to the unaided eye of reason? It was a primary part of Kant's
purpose to settle such disputes once and for all, and in his *Critique of
Pure Reason* he undertook to demonstrate that neither reason nor
sensory experience was by itself sufficient for the acquisition of
knowledge: both were essential. According to Kant, it was true that
human cognition necessarily conformed to an underlying framework of
a priori forms and concepts which were imposed by the mind upon the
data supplied by the senses; at the same time, the legitimate
application of these was confined to the sensory sphere and any
attempt to extend them to establish truths concerning what obtained
outside that sphere must always be unjustified. In the light of this, Kant
drew a firm line between hypotheses of the sort put forward in the
natural sciences, which were susceptible to confirmation by experiment
and observation, and theories which purported to make cognitive

claims about a supersensible or transcendent order of things that lay beyond the range of such procedures. Claims of the latter kind belonged to 'dogmatic' or speculative metaphysics, an 'old and sophistical mock-science' whose pretensions he believed himself to have shown finally to be empty and without warrant. As he put it elsewhere: 'All knowledge of things out of mere pure understanding or pure reason is nothing but illusion, and only in experience is truth.'

Although they were elaborated within the context of an argument of striking originality and power, Kant's objections to the pursuit of speculative metaphysics were, broadly speaking, consonant with ones that had already been formulated by David Hume (1711–76). Furthermore and again like Hume, he realized that they entailed consequences which were of more than merely academic interest. For they apparently impinged, with destructive effect, upon the various efforts that had been made over the centuries to prove propositions fundamental to the Christian religion, above all those concerning the existence and nature of God: in Kant's opinion, it unquestionably followed from his criticisms that 'all attempts to make a purely speculative use of reason in reference to theology are entirely fruitless and of their inner nature null and void'. Even so, there were significant differences between the two thinkers as to the morals that should be drawn from the failure of such attempts. Hume's response to 'the imperfections of natural reason' in this domain was one of sceptical irony and found characteristic expression in a well-known passage of his *Enquiry Concerning Human Understanding* in which he implied that no reasonable individual could sincerely endorse the doctrines of Christianity without being conscious of 'a continued miracle in his own person'. By comparison, Kant's reaction was both more complex and less dismissive and was epitomized in his claim – by no means ironical in intent – that he had found it necessary to deny knowledge in order to make room for faith. What did this somewhat cryptic assertion amount to?

Whatever confusions Kant may have discerned in the projects of speculative metaphysicians, he should not be understood as thereby wishing to rule out of court the very conception of a supersensible realm; indeed, his own 'transcendental idealism', in which a distinction was drawn between the empirical world of phenomenal objects or 'appearances' and a 'noumenal' world of things in themselves that was inaccessible to experience, can be said to have presupposed it. What he did maintain was that nothing whatsoever at the theoretical level could be *known* about such a realm. Thus the cognitive claims of speculative theology, inasmuch as they purported to provide us with demonstrable truths concerning the supersensible, were certainly unacceptable; but so, too, were the arguments of those who contended that it was possible conclusively to demonstrate their falsity: in this respect the atheist was no better off than the theist. There was hence a sense in which Kant considered that his position at least protected the tenets of religious faith from the assaults of 'dogmatic' criticism. But he also believed that it was open to him to take a further step in their defence. This involved switching attention from the speculative or theoretical use of reason to its practical use, and for him that meant taking account of the presuppositions of the moral consciousness; it was there that reason under its practical aspect directly manifested itself.

From one point of view Kant's ethical theory can be seen as presenting an alternative to naturalistic approaches to morality of a kind favoured by many Enlightenment writers and of which a psychological version had been propounded by Hume himself. Kant did not, for example, accept Hume's suggestion that all behaviour, together with the standards in terms of which it was morally assessed, must ultimately be explained or interpreted by reference to the passions and desires of mankind. He thought that trying in this way to base moral choice and evaluation upon contingent wants and sentiments was tantamount to reducing them to something purely subjective and susceptible to inevitable variations. But such a conception of their status was at odds with the entrenched conviction that fundamental moral laws possessed universal validity, binding upon all persons irrespective of empirical circumstances and independently of individual preferences or proclivities; the mere recognition that it conflicted with our inexpungeable intuitions about the objective requirements of morality was alone sufficient to render it implausible. It did not follow, however, that we should revert instead to the time-honoured opinion that these requirements derived their validity from the alleged fact that they expressed the will of God and embodied his commands. Notions of the latter sort, at least as traditionally understood, were deeply antipathetic to Kant: apart from other objections to which they stood exposed, they implied that the individual must submit to the judgement and direction of an external authority, thereby sacrificing his autonomy and independence as a rational agent in his own right. And it was precisely in the exercise of rationality that Kant conceived the essence of moral thought and action to reside. That reason may play a subordinate role in behaviour, merely indicating the means to the fulfilment of natural desires and aims, he had no wish to deny; he insisted, none the less, that what distinguished us in our capacity as moral beings was the ability to act in defiance of the promptings of 'sensuous' inclination and to be determined in what we did solely by principles which we ourselves prescribed. To the extent that such principles were not grounded on empirical considerations but were subject instead to the purely formal condition that they could be consistently endorsed as one which everybody should obey, they might be said to derive from reason alone and hence to impose obligations that were necessarily acceptable to all rational agents. And in following out what he believed to be the full implications of this doctrine Kant developed a theory which seemed, not merely to identify the claims of morality with the categorical demands of duty, but also to assimilate the latter to the deliverances of an autonomous rationality that wholly transcended the sphere of natural feeling and desire.

At first glance it might appear that Kant's insistence upon the primacy of reason as a source of ethical requirements entailed the logical independence of morality from religion. It undoubtedly involved the rejection of a theologically based ethics in the traditional sense; there could be no question of invoking the commands of a deity as a means of authenticating moral rules. There was, however, another possibility to be considered. For the relation between the two might be the reverse of what it was commonly supposed to be, morality affording support to religious belief rather than the other way about. With this in mind Kant argued that there were certain convictions, inseparable from the 'interest' of pure reason in its practical or moral capacity, in which ideas concerning the supersensible played an essential part. One of these involved the notion of freedom. It seemed to him clear that the conception we have of ourselves as responsible moral agents presupposed a capacity for rational choice which could not be ascribed to us if our actions were exclusively determined by natural causality. But this assumption could never be justified if we supposed ourselves to be merely members of the empirical order of nature, in which (on his view) everything was subject to causal laws; the adoption of the moral standpoint therefore required us to believe that there was an aspect of our existence that could not be captured in empirical terms and for Kant this meant thinking of ourselves as belonging to the noumenal or 'intelligible' world of things in themselves as well as to the phenomenal world of sensory experience. Nor was this all. Apart from its commitment to the freedom of the will, he maintained that morality had implications which were of more specific relevance to the fundamental tenets of religion. Thus he suggested that in our moral thought we were aware of a duty to promote what he called the *summum bonum*, the 'highest good', and also of an associated obligation to pursue our moral perfection as individuals. So far as the first was concerned, the good in question required for its ultimate realization a state of affairs in which happiness was justly apportioned to moral desert; it was evident, however, that this was not a situation which – people and things being as they were – we could conceivably hope to bring about purely on our own. Nevertheless, since it presented itself to us as something we were morally obliged to further, its achievement must be regarded as attainable and in Kant's opinion that demanded the postulation of a supersensible agency capable of ensuring that our efforts would not be vain: as he put it in his *Critique of Practical Reason*, 'the highest good is possible in the world only on the supposition of a supreme cause of nature', and this – in so far as it acted 'through understanding and will' – could only be God. On similar lines, he argued that the obligation to attain moral perfection was not something that an individual could ever expect to fulfil within the contingencies of an earthly existence; it was therefore necessary for him to postulate one that transcended these limits and in which 'endless progress' towards such perfection could be made. In religious terms, that amounted to assuming the immortality of the soul.

In putting forward such considerations, Kant was emphatic that the existence of God, freedom, and immortality could only be established from 'a practical point of view'. From a theoretical standpoint they could be neither proved nor disproved; in other words, there could be no knowledge here of the kind we have in the case of, say, scientific or mathematical truths. Furthermore, he had no wish to be understood as offering a philosophical underpinning to historical beliefs in the reality of divinely appointed persons or supernatural occurrences of the sort often invoked in support of religious claims; so far as he was concerned, scriptural accounts which seemed to transgress the limits of rational credibility had to be interpreted in an allegorical rather than a literal fashion and should be treated as providing 'incentives' to what were essentially moral ideals. 'Making room for faith' in the sense he had in mind did not mean trying to rehabilitate contentions which had been stigmatized by a host of Enlightenment critics as 'superstition'. On the contrary, it was a 'faith of pure practical reason', securely founded in the authoritative deliverances of the moral consciousness, that he sought to legitimize; nothing less would do.

Or so at least it seemed. Yet to some of Kant's readers his arguments appeared to betray an ambivalence of intention which left their real import unclear. Thus there were certainly times when he was prepared to speak of the beliefs allegedly implicit in our moral aspirations as 'extending' our insight in a way that entitled us to make positive affirmations about matters which necessarily lay beyond the reach of theoretical investigation. But his assertions to this effect were apparently qualified by other passages where he could be taken to be implying, more guardedly and perhaps more sceptically, that the beliefs in question were of subjective significance only. Though presupposed by our ethical thinking, they could not on that account be accredited with objective validity: what propositions the ethical standpoint committed us to was one thing, whether they were actually true was another, and while they might represent convictions that were integral to the adoption of that standpoint, any certainty they thereby acquired was 'not logical, but moral'. In some places, indeed, he explicitly wrote as if the faith whose claims to acceptance he wished to endorse was a matter of the will rather than of the intellect. And this seemed to point towards a very different conception of its status.

One may suspect that such ambiguities were in part deliberate and that Kant himself was conscious of tensions in his thought which he was unable satisfactorily to resolve. But however that may be, there can be no doubt that he brought into prominence considerations that were to exercise a profound and enduring influence upon subsequent approaches to the problem of defining the nature and standing of religious belief. To many of his successors it at least appeared evident that he had finally dispelled all hope of providing a rational justification of theological claims along orthodox lines. Even so, he had not been content to leave matters there; and his own appeal to the asseverations of moral experience, whatever obscurities and uncertainties it might otherwise involve, was nevertheless felt by some to be suggestive of a fresh perspective within which religious ideas and aspirations could be understood. It seemed possible, in other words, that attention might profitably be shifted from a theoretical preoccupation with the cognitive validity of religious belief to a more fruitful concern with the nature of the subjective consciousness from which such belief arose. Two philosophers who may be said – though in very different ways – to have given expression to this altered outlook were J. G. Fichte (1762–1814) and F. D. E. Schleiermacher (1768–1834). In the case of the former Kant's stress upon the ethical dimension of the religious standpoint was reiterated, while at the same time being accorded a radical twist. Thus, in an essay entitled *On the Foundation of our Belief in a Divine Government of the Universe*, Fichte went out of his way to dismiss as misguided all attempts to ground the existence of the world upon the notion of an intelligent author or cause. The concept of God as a 'separate entity' or quasi-personal agency was an unthinkable one, defying coherent analysis. It should be replaced by the conception of a 'moral world order' to which we necessarily belonged as practical beings and in which we could be sure that good actions would infallibly succeed and evil ones just as certainly fail: belief in such an order was, moreover, a 'fundamental presupposition' of the moral consciousness and on this account did not admit of argument or demonstration. For Schleiermacher, on the other hand, the source of religion was to be found, not in the sphere of autonomous ethical conviction, but rather in a shared feeling of dependence upon a divine reality that was itself unknowable and beyond the reach of conceptual thought. Both writers, however, were agreed in confining themselves to the articulation of what they believed to be essential to the religious consciousness and in disclaiming any pretensions to offer a theoretical substantiation of its presumed objects. Whatever else might be said about the latter, they did not fall within the range of rational enquiry.

Hegel's system

How far, though, were such subjectively orientated approaches really adequate as a means of coming to terms with religion from a philosophical point of view? There was one major German thinker who considered that they were not and who undertook to demonstrate that the fundamental tenets of Christianity might after all be understood in a

5. Georg Wilhelm Friedrich Hegel (1770–1831).

sense that showed them to be a repository of objective truth. This was G. W. F. Hegel (1770–1831).

Hegel was from the outset of his intellectual career deeply preoccupied with determining the status of religious belief. As his early unpublished manuscripts indicate, he was at first inclined to adopt a standpoint that was in some ways reminiscent of Kant's. Thus he initially referred to morality as constituting 'the end and essence of all religion', Jesus himself being portrayed as propounding a Kantian-style ethic which was finally subject to nothing beyond the free exercise of 'universal reason'. At the same time, however, he exhibited a profoundly sceptical attitude to the dogmas of theology, the latter being said to involve claims which defied rational credence and which were founded upon an ultimately unacceptable deference to external 'authority'. It is therefore not surprising that Hegel's extensive criticisms of what he called the 'positivity' of latter-day institutionalized Christianity, encompassing both the doctrines and the practices of an authoritarian Church, should have been associated by some of his commentators with the attacks which anticlerical representatives of the Enlightenment had typically directed against the Christian religion. Yet such appearances were in important respects deceptive. Even at this stage his tone was not so much one of detached irony or ridicule as of personal dissatisfaction; and in the subsequent development of his thought he increasingly tended to treat theological doctrines as creations of the human spirit which demanded careful and sympathetic investigation – they could not be simply written off on the ground that they were the absurd products of antiquated ignorance and superstition. In the words of a significant manuscript written in 1800, the time had come to 'deduce this now repudiated dogmatics out of . . . the needs of human nature and thus to show its naturalness and its necessity'. In part, this meant interpreting religion as an historical phenomenon which was expressive of the potentialities of the human mind at different stages of its evolution. But, as was later to transpire, Hegel's interest in the history of religious ideas was not confined to the sphere of empirical understanding and research; it had a further aspect whose importance can only be appreciated in the context of his metaphysics. For in his mature writings he came to view religion as a mode of consciousness that had progressed to a point from which it could be seen to reflect certain fundamental insights into the nature of reality as a whole. It was his contention, moreover, that the true implications of these insights finally became apparent within the framework of his own philosophy, where they were presented in a perspicuous and rationally accessible form.

The emergence of the famous Hegelian 'system', which was to brood like an all-pervasive presence over so much of Kierkegaard's work, can thus be said to have been in one sense continuous with the development of its author's religious preoccupations. It would none the less be an error to assume that it was constructed with the object of reinstating orthodox attempts to provide a philosophical justification of theological dogmas. For Hegel believed that, as traditionally understood, these dogmas were themselves symptomatic of oppositions inherent in our thought and knowledge which it was the task of his own philosophy to overcome. To grasp why he believed this we must glance briefly at the outlines of that philosophy as it eventually took shape.

Hegel's system involved a radical and quite explicit departure from certain familiar ways of envisaging the natural and social worlds in which we live. At the everyday or commonsense level (he thought) we regard the realm of nature as something apart from ourselves, enjoying a wholly independent existence. Furthermore, we may also approach other persons, whether individually or collectively, as separate beings to whom we are related in a purely external way. In his opinion, this was prone to raise problems both from a theoretical and from a practical standpoint. Theoretically, the world may appear to us as ultimately lying beyond our cognitive grasp; such a picture had haunted previous philosophical attempts to characterize the extent of human knowledge and had found most recent expression in the Kantian claims that ultimate reality consisted of unknowable 'things in themselves', these being divided by an unbridgeable gulf from the contents of human thought and consciousness. Practically, there are times when people are apt to experience a sense of estrangement from the societies to which they belong and in the context of which they pursue their various aims and purposes. In such a condition, which Hegel termed one of 'alienation', the individual is caused to think of himself as an isolated particular, thrown back upon his own resources and excogitating principles of action that are grounded upon nothing but the convictions of his private judgement or will. And here again we may be reminded of certain aspects of the Kantian philosophy; in this case, those that concerned the alleged autonomy of the moral agent who was portrayed as being finally dependent upon no more than the deliverances of his own rational nature or 'noumenal' self.

Whatever may have been his original attitude to Kant's ethics, Hegel later criticized it as echoing tensions and divisions of a kind that recurred at different stages of human experience and which were productive, both cognitively and morally, of dissatisfaction and disquiet. How did these arise and how could they be overcome? The solution lay in an interpretation of reality which invoked the notion of 'absolute spirit', or *Geist*. From a Hegelian point of view what confronts us as being apparently foreign or 'other' is in fact the expression of an all-encompassing cosmic process in which we ourselves participate and whose underlying essence is spiritual or mental.

Thus in his logical theory Hegel undertook to demonstrate that the innermost truth of things – 'as it is, without husk' – could be presented in terms of universal categories of thought that unfolded according to 'dialectically' necessary laws; and in his philosophies of nature and of history he sought to show how spirit, which originally externalized itself in the shape of an unconscious natural realm, subsequently came to a gradual realization of its fundamental character through the developing consciousness of human beings. This arose at two levels. At the practical level, it manifested itself in the emergence of successive historical societies, leading to the creation of a type of rationally ordered community with whose objective institutions the individual could subjectively identify and to whose moral requirements he would willingly subscribe – the framework of rules and duties imposed would be seen by him to coincide with his own essential interests as an agent seeking fulfilment as a free and rational being. At the level of reflective thought, the world would come to be viewed as the product of a mind whose underlying structure was mirrored in our own thinking processes: in Hegel's words, it was 'the aim of knowledge . . . to divest the objective world that stands opposed to us of its strangeness, and, as the phrase is, to find ourselves at home in it; which means no more than to trace the objective world back to the notion – to our innermost self'. Reality, that is to say, would no longer appear to us as something irreducibly independent and external, and spirit, through the medium of human consciousness, would arrive at a complete and satisfying understanding of itself.

Hegel implied indeed that this desirable consummation had been achieved in his own philosophy. Amongst other things, he had given an account of the ways in which human thought progresses through a series of partial and inadequate approximations to the status of what he called 'absolute knowledge'. And in the course of doing so he believed that he had managed to bring to light the inner or concealed meaning of religion. For religious conceptions as they historically evolved could be seen to exhibit a developing insight into the spiritual significance of the world, an insight that attained its highest form in Christianity – the 'absolute religion'. In his opinion, however, it was vital to realize that the insight in question had been formulated in figurative or mythical terms. Taken literally and at their face value, religious doctrines were rationally unacceptable; moreover, they were apt to lead to radical misunderstandings. The conception of God, for example, as a transcendent being to whom human beings stand in an external relation of dependence was a reflection on the theological plane of a mode of thinking which Hegel's approach was expressly designed to supersede; associated with an historical outlook which he referred to in his *Phenomenology of Mind* as 'the unhappy consciousness', it involved the projection into an unearthly 'beyond' of potentialities that human beings, as vehicles of spirit, were destined to realize at the level of earthly existence. It was certainly no part of his purpose to rehabilitate, let alone try to justify, such ideas. When properly understood, on the other hand, religious beliefs could be regarded as giving pictorial expression to matters that had been conceptually articulated and substantiated in his own theory: thus the Christian doctrines of the fall and of subsequent redemption through the incarnation of Christ were susceptible to an interpretation that showed them to be consonant with Hegel's notion of the manner in which spirit overcame internal divisions, ultimately returning to itself and achieving complete fulfilment and comprehension of its nature through man. In this sense

Christianity was not, or not merely, a matter of subjective faith, practical or otherwise. Correctly viewed, its contents could be seen to be rationally acceptable and objectively valid. Hence it had, to all appearances, found a final and secure resting-place within the hospitable walls of the Hegelian system. Reason and religion had been reconciled.

But at what price? What did it really mean to assert that the contents of Christianity and Hegelianism were the same? Some of the master's more radically minded followers, who came to be known as the Young Hegelians, took it upon themselves to elicit what they believed to be the actual implications of this claim. In his extremely influential *Life of Jesus* (1835) D. F. Strauss (1808–74) presented a critical account of the Gospel stories in which he argued that they must be evaluated in a way that paid due attention to 'the spirit of the ancient world and of the people of that time'. The notion of a 'God-man' who mysteriously combined supernatural and human attributes was the product of a mentality which could only express its underlying vision in a concrete and quasi-historical form. Looked at from the higher standpoint of philosophy, however, and stripped of its mythological trappings, the Christian doctrine of the incarnation should be read as symbolizing the essential unity of the spiritual and the natural in the life and development of the human species as a whole. Thus the dualism that beset the traditional dogmas of religious belief, according to which God and man belonged to separate spheres of existence, must be replaced by the insight that it was through humanity alone that the 'divine essence' could be realized. God and man were in fact one; and from this it was a short step to the contention – explicitly advanced by Ludwig Feuerbach 1804–72) – that the God of religion was no more than the externalization, in an imaginary and idealized form, of man's own nature and fundamental attributes. The conception of a divinity set over against the world and demanding worship and obedience was an illusion, a 'dream of the human mind'; man's supposed knowledge of God amounted in the end to no more than man's knowledge of himself. Hence the Hegelian

6. *Christ Blessing the Children*, an image of Christ in all his humanity. The secret of theology had finally been shown to be anthropology.

aspiration to vindicate the claims of religion in rational terms had apparently reached its culmination in a theory that entailed their virtual supersession. As Feuerbach himself succinctly put it, the secret of theology had finally been shown to be anthropology.

Chapter 3
The immorality of an age

Kierkegaard's reaction to the developments described in the last chapter was a complex one. As he made abundantly clear in various of his writings, he fully appreciated the devastating objections which Kant had brought against the project of trying to prove by theoretical means the fundamental tenets of Christian orthodoxy. What, on the other hand, seemed to him to be quite unacceptable were the different attempts that had been made to resolve the issues that Kant's critical philosophy had left in its wake. For, in one way or another, these amounted to endeavours to guarantee the reasonableness of Christian belief along lines that involved at best its emasculation and at worst its total transformation.

Kierkegaard in fact showed himself to be far from unsympathetic to Kant's original insistence that religious convictions were a matter, not of knowledge, but of faith; this was indeed an aspect of the Kantian approach which he was subsequently to explore in his own individual fashion and at considerable length. It was, however, another thing to suggest – as Kant himself had gone on to do – that the limitations of theoretical or cognitive reason could somehow be circumvented by an appeal to reason in its ethical capacity. The contention that beliefs in God and in personal immortality were, as 'postulates of practical reason', necessarily presupposed by the moral consciousness was tantamount to treating morality rather than religion as the central object of human concern; furthermore, it was a corollary of this position that it set the historical aspects of Christianity in a perspective which tended to accord them a purely peripheral significance. And far from being met, such difficulties were (if anything) accentuated by the Hegelian aspiration to demonstrate that religion was susceptible of an interpretation which showed it to be after all a repository of objective truth. The claim that religious ideas should be construed as expressing, at a primitive and mythical stage of thinking, a content whose hidden import awaited formulation within the framework of an all-embracing metaphysical system might have found acceptance amongst a number of contemporary theologians. Yet in Kierkegaard's eyes it meant in effect a radical revision of the Christian message, this being finally replaced by an entirely different set of principles. Thus, whatever might have been Hegel's own express intentions, there was at least a sense in which the writers of the Young Hegelian school displayed a more perceptive grasp of the underlying tenor of his thought than those who welcomed it as providing a rational substantiation of traditional teachings. The gap between metaphysical idealism and humanistic atheism might at first glance seem a wide one; it was not, however, difficult to discern how the transition had been made, once references to the activities of concrete human beings had been substituted for Hegel's mystifyingly abstract allusions to the workings of absolute spirit.

Even so, there were sophisticated Danish thinkers – such as Kierkegaard's one-time tutor, Martensen – who had been deeply impressed by 'the latest German philosophy' and who maintained that Christian orthodoxy had nothing to fear from its implications. In their view this philosophy, far from threatening the cherished truths of religion, demonstrated how they could be both preserved intact and at the same time fully harmonized with the demands of reason by invoking the mediating categories of the Hegelian system. Hence the question presented itself as to how such a radical misconception had arisen and acquired widespread currency. In part the answer lay in a failure to

7. Immanuel Kant (1724–1804).

comprehend the structure of the system itself and in part in a failure to recognize what Christianity, properly conceived, involved. Both failures, however, were rooted in a pervasive incapacity to come to grips with something which Kierkegaard believed to be of more fundamental significance and which therefore called for prior consideration. In his own words:

> My principal thought was that in our age, because of the great increase of knowledge, we had forgotten what it means to *exist*, and what *inwardness* signifies, and that the misunderstanding between speculative philosophy and Christianity was explicable on that ground. I now resolved to go back as far as possible, in order not to reach the religious mode of existence too soon, to say nothing of the specifically Christian mode of existence ... If men had forgotten what it means to exist religiously, they had doubtless also forgotten what it means to exist as human beings; this must therefore be set forth. But above all it must

8. A ventriloquist. Kierkegaard remarked that a species of 'ventriloquism' had developed; people took refuge in a depersonalized realm of ideas and doctrines rather than confronting the fact that everyone is finally accountable to himself for his life, character, and outlook.

not be done in a dogmatising manner, for then the misunderstanding would instantly take the explanatory effort to itself in a new misunderstanding, as if existing consisted in getting to know something about this or that.

(CUP 223)

At first sight it may seem puzzling to be told that we can forget what it means to exist, as if existence were something we can intelligibly be said to engage in or undergo, like swimming or having a headache. And it is certainly true that in more recent times many of Kierkegaard's existentialist successors have not been averse to discussing the concept in ways liable to cause justifiable perplexity. In the present context, however, there seems to be nothing in what he says that need occasion logical unease. His point is a relatively unproblematic one and concerns the manner in which he believed the majority of his contemporaries were prone to think of themselves and to lead their lives. Thus he considered that they had succumbed to an impersonal and anonymous mode of consciousness which precluded spontaneous feeling and was devoid of a secure sense of self-identity. Everything tended to be seen in 'abstract' terms, as theoretical possibilities which could be contemplated and compared but to the concrete realization of which people were unwilling to commit themselves. If they attended to their own attitudes or emotions it was through a thick haze of pseudo-scientific expressions or cliché-ridden phrases which they had picked up from books or newspapers rather than in the direct light of their own inner experience. Living had become a matter of knowing rather than doing, accumulating information and learning things by rote as opposed to taking decisions that bore the stamp of individual passion or conviction. What this led to was the formation of an outlook in which everything was approached through the medium of set responses and automatic reactions; people knew what they were supposed to say, but they no longer attached any real significance to the words they used. As Kierkegaard wrote in the long section of *A Literary Review* entitled 'The Present Age':

In fact there are handbooks for everything, and very soon education, all the world over, will consist in learning a greater or lesser number of comments by heart, and people will excel according to their capacity for singling out the various facts like a printer singling out the letters, but completely ignorant of the meaning of anything.

(PA 88–9)

Moreover, these trends were accompanied by a propensity to identify with amorphous abstract entities like 'humanity' or 'the public', people thereby absolving themselves from individual responsibility for what they thought and said. To put it crudely, there was safety in numbers: 'everyone can have an opinion; but they have to band together numerically in order to have one' (PA 91). And somewhat similar considerations applied at the level of practical behaviour. People were ready enough to talk of doing things 'on principle', but they were apt to treat the principles they appealed to as if they were endowed with a purely external or impersonal authority, unrelated to the agent's own preferences and concerns; in this sense, one could 'do anything "on principle" and avoid all personal responsibility' (PA 85). As Kierkegaard remarked elsewhere, 'no man, none, dares to say *I*'; instead, a species of 'ventriloquism' had become *de rigueur* – the ordinary person had become a mouthpiece of public opinion, the professor a mouthpiece of theoretical speculation, the pastor a mouthpiece of religious meditation. All were in different ways submissive to abstractions to which they attributed an independent reality. Rather than confront the fact that everyone is finally accountable to himself for his life, character, and outlook, they took refuge in a depersonalized realm of reified ideas and doctrines.

It is against the background of such alleged tendencies, which he stigmatized as constituting 'the specific immorality of the age', that Kierkegaard's particular mode of conceiving his task has to be viewed. The period, as he never tired of repeating, was one of passionless reflection and detached understanding. It would be a mistake to suppose that he was therefore opposed to objective enquiry as such, though this charge has sometimes been made against him. The methodical and collaborative pursuit of disinterested knowledge was perfectly justified when carried out within its proper limits, as in the case of the historical and natural sciences. Confusion and self-deception arose, however, when people allowed the attitudes appropriate to such pursuit to impinge upon matters that lay outside its true domain. For in so doing they lost sight of themselves as unique individuals and were content to adopt a contemplative or observational stance from which everything appeared under the aspect of bland generalities and the bloodless universals of collective thought. Considerations that rightfully belonged to the sphere of personal experience and involvement were thereby transposed into an external two-dimensional setting of 'representational ideas', human activities being subsumed beneath comprehensive conceptions which emptied them of intrinsic value and robbed them of any significance they might possess from the subjective standpoints of the agents concerned: the situation (Kierkegaard suggested) might be compared with that of someone who, wishing to travel in Denmark, consulted a small-scale map of Europe – the map showed him where Denmark stood in relation to other parts of the world but it told him nothing that was relevant to his purpose. Such an ethos had affected not only current attitudes to morality, but also those adopted towards religion. At the level of everyday consciousness and behaviour religious beliefs were entertained in a purely nominal or abstract way, with no reference to the concrete contexts of practical choice that would lend them life and meaning; while at the hands of philosophers and theologians they had been translated into the language of theoretical speculation and treated as if they were answerable to objectively conceived standards of truth that wholly transcended the subjective needs and points of view of particular human beings.

How should these misapprehensions be countered? One course that might naturally suggest itself was that of simply seeking to correct, in a straightforward and reasoned fashion, certain mistaken beliefs and assumptions. In the present case, however, Kierkegaard maintained that to follow such a procedure was to be in danger of missing what was really at issue. Certainly it would be the appropriate line to take if the matter were merely one of questioning a purely theoretical position or thesis. But what was at stake here was something more fundamental than a particular set of cognitive claims. Rather, it was a pervasive way of looking at things and it had its source in an attitude to life from which a person could not be dislodged by intellectual argument alone. What was required – in the first instance, at least – was to bring home to people what 'it means for you and me and him, each for himself, to be human beings', and this involved leading them to recognize for themselves, through an appeal to their own inner experience, the considerations that actuated them in adopting a particular mode of living and the limitations it imposed. Such an enlargement of an individual's self-understanding and critical self-awareness could not be achieved by abstract instruction or the inculcation of salutary precepts: it might, however, be assisted by entering imaginatively into his or her point of view, empathetically eliciting its emotional foundations and practical implications while at the same time exhibiting how these diverged from those implicit in alternative outlooks or approaches. By following such a method, which he termed one of 'indirect communication' and which was Socratic in inspiration, he sought to enable his readers to acquire a more perspicuous insight into their own situation and motivation, but without the didacticism that was characteristic of 'objective' modes of discourse. His aim was not, in other words, to add to the sum of their propositional knowledge in the manner of a schoolmaster or an academic teacher, nor did he purport to 'compel a person to accept an opinion, a conviction, a belief' in the autocratic style of some privileged authority. On the contrary, the idea was to approach people 'from behind', manoeuvring them into a position from which they themselves, as a result of interior reflection, could step back and make a radical choice between remaining where they were and opting for a fundamental change. Their freedom and autonomy as individuals must at all costs be respected; it was ultimately for them to decide what to do, what course to follow, once they had arrived at a deep and unclouded comprehension of the implications of contrasting life-views. But it was an essential precondition of this that they should be clear about the nature and limits of their own positions. As Kierkegaard was at pains to stress, persons in the grip of a particular outlook were only too apt to deceive themselves into supposing that no other options lay open, tending to interpret whatever was presented to them in a fashion that conformed to its requirements.

Kierkegaard maintained that it was in the light of this project that the initial stage of his literary production, comprising his so-called 'aesthetic' works, had been undertaken. Here, though, a cautionary note may be sounded. When, later on, in his posthumously published *The Point of View of my Work as an Author* (1859), he offered a retrospective account of his object in writing the books in question, he spoke as if he had been guided all along by a specifically religious interest; his cardinal aim had been one of divesting people of the illusion that they were Christians, an illusion which – at that stage at least – he appeared mainly to associate with the acceptance of what he termed an 'aesthetic' approach to life. In his own words, 'an illusion can never be destroyed directly, and only by indirect means can it be radically removed' (PV 24). It is not clear, however, that what he said in the above context accurately reflected his earlier concerns; one may legitimately wonder whether his later conception of himself as having a providential mission, of being 'like a spy in a higher service', may not have caused him to oversimplify and even distort the character of his original preoccupations. This is a point that has been remarked upon by critics and it is one we shall have to return to. But first we must look at the actual content of some of the relevant literature, leaving the question of its true place in his development until afterwards.

Chapter 4
Modes of existence

There can certainly be no dispute that all the early 'aesthetic' works – *Either/Or*, *Repetition*, *Fear and Trembling*, and *Stages on Life's Way* – exemplify the 'indirect' approach to which Kierkegaard attached such importance. Not only do they set out to present opposed outlooks and styles of living; they do this in an imaginative or 'poetical' fashion which is designed to exhibit – from the inside – what it is like to envisage life within the perspectives identified. The reader is invited to participate vicariously in these contrasting visions, much as he might if he were entering into the minds of characters portrayed in a novel or a play. The fictional analogy is, indeed, apposite in more than one way, Kierkegaard never addressing the reader directly, as the author, but instead speaking to him through the medium of different pseudonyms under which the books were published; by adopting such masks and shifting disguises he appeared to distance himself, if sometimes rather disingenuously, from the positions to which his pseudonyms or invented personages variously subscribed. This served a dual purpose: it was designed to convey in an intimate manner the distinctive flavour and texture of disparate life-views; at the same time, it left the reader to draw his own practical conclusions from what was communicated to him – the various outlooks were allowed to 'speak for themselves', no external attempt being made to arbitrate or decide between them.

What form did they take? Kierkegaard distinguishes three basic modes or 'spheres' of existence: the aesthetic, the ethical, and the religious. Although allusions to all of them are to be found, in one shape or another, in each of the books mentioned, the contrast between the aesthetic and the ethical comes out most clearly in *Either/Or* and that between the ethical and the religious in *Fear and Trembling*; attention can therefore be focused on the latter works. Even so, the three categories Kierkegaard introduces are in certain respects deceptively wide-ranging, and what they cover is more autobiographical in content than his favoured method of presentation would suggest. In each case the attitudes comprised show considerable variations, reflecting not only his perception of contemporary cultural trends but also the complex patterns of his own history and development; indeed, some of the material was drawn directly from his journals. Thus traces of the psychological difficulties and dilemmas of his student years, including those connected with his ambivalent relationship with his father, are frequently discernible; so, too, are the traumatic repercussions of his broken engagement to Regine Olsen, Kierkegaard making oblique references to it which she was intended to read and understand. This lends to parts of the writing a rather contrived air which has evoked a sympathetic response from some of his modern votaries but which has produced a cooler reaction amongst more critically inclined commentators. In any event, it certainly informs a good deal of what he has to say about the relations between the different outlooks that are portrayed.

The aesthetic and the ethical

Either/Or is by any standards a remarkable book, and it is not surprising that it was greeted with a kind of bemused fascination when it first appeared. The aesthetic and ethical standpoints are presented in the form of edited sets of papers and letters. The papers are ascribed to a representative of the aesthetic position, referred to as 'A', and the letters to an older person, 'B': the latter, who is the protagonist of the ethical and whose communications are addressed to A, is said by the fictitious editor to have been by profession a judge. A's papers seem at first sight almost calculated to arouse puzzlement; they display a dazzling variety of styles and deal with assorted topics that often appear to be only loosely related to one another. Thus they range from scattered aphorisms and personal observations to reflective discussion of tragedy (the *Antigone*), opera and the erotic (Mozart's *Don Giovanni*), and Goethe's treatment of the Faust legend, and they conclude with a protracted account, in the form of a diary, of a minutely planned and cerebrally conceived seduction; the last (as Kierkegaard wryly noted later) may have been partly responsible for the book's initial success. The diffuseness and apparent lack of determinate direction of this section of the work, which were perhaps intended to mirror problems inherent in A's point of view, contrast sharply with the form taken by its second half. Here we are offered two, extremely lengthy, epistles by B. Written in a sober and deliberate prose, they give the impression of being designed to throw into relief the effervescent and rather self-conscious 'brilliance' of their supposed recipient. At the same time, they serve to illustrate – through the various criticisms which the judge makes of A's position – what lies behind Kierkegaard's use of the terms 'aesthetic' and 'ethical' to identify opposed outlooks and modes of living. To some extent this emerges from the long disquisition on the significance of marriage which is the subject of the first letter; it is, however, in B's second communication, the well-known 'Equilibrium between the Aesthetic and the Ethical in the Composition of the Personality', that what Kierkegaard has in mind receives general and comprehensive expression.

Some writers have interpreted the division in question in terms of more familiar theoretical contrasts: hedonism and conventional morality, for example, or the Kantian distinction between sensuous inclination and the imperative requirements of reason. Echoes of both are certainly present in a number of the judge's remarks. None the less, 'Equilibrium' is a rich and involved piece of writing where a multitude of ideas are to be found densely, and at times confusingly, crowded together;

consequently, such simple dichotomies as those proposed provide at best an inadequate guide. Although, early on in the judge's letter, the main interest and object of the aesthetic mode of life is said to consist in enjoyment, it quickly becomes apparent that this is by no means a complete or exhaustive characterization. 'Aestheticism', as understood in Kierkegaard's generous and in some ways idiosyncratic sense, can take on different guises: it manifests itself at diverse levels of sophistication and self-consciousness and it ramifies in directions beyond those of a mere pursuit of pleasure for pleasure's sake; indeed, what he says about it is more frequently reminiscent of 19th-century Romantic attitudes than the rather mundane hedonism associated with much 18th-century philosophical literature. Similarly with the 'ethical'. Here there is undoubtedly talk of the importance of determinate duties and responsibilities; but we should misconstrue Kierkegaard's overall conception if we assumed that it could be reduced, either to a mere observance of socially recognized rules, or alternatively to a Kantian respect for the deliverances of pure practical reason. Not only is the truth more complex and less straightforward than these limited interpretations suggest; it also has significant points of contact with other, more far-reaching, implications of his position.

Let us then consider the matter in more detail, beginning with the case of the aesthetic individual. Despite Kierkegaard's explicit claim that there is 'no didacticism' in *Either/Or* (CUP 228), it is arguable that he does not really confine himself to presenting two rival viewpoints, leaving the question of which is finally to be preferred entirely to the reader. For one thing, the ethicist is given the second, and therefore the last, word. For another, we are given the impression that B has, in some fundamental sense, seen through A's attitude; he grasps its motivation and is thereby enabled to criticize it in a way that undermines it. Thus, as the judge proceeds, it becomes clear that the condition of such a person is regarded by him as being in certain crucial respects a pathological one. Of these, two in particular stand out and can be seen to be connected.

In the first place, it is indicated that the man who lives aesthetically is not really in control, either of himself or his situation. He typically exists *ins Blaue hinein*; he tends to live 'for the moment', for whatever the passing instant will bring in the way of entertainment, excitement, interest. Committed to nothing permanent or definite, dispersed in sensuous 'immediacy', he may do or think one thing at a given time, the exact opposite at some other; his life is therefore without 'continuity', lacks stability or focus, changes course according to mood or circumstance, is 'like a witch's letter from which one sense can be got now and then another, depending on how one turns it'. Even so, it should not be inferred that such a man is always or necessarily governed by mere impulse; on the contrary, he may be reflective and calculating, like the seducer whose diary is included amongst A's papers. If, however, he does adopt long-term goals or decide to follow certain maxims, it is in a purely 'experimental' spirit: he will continue only for so long as the idea appeals to him, the alternative of giving up if he gets tired or bored, or if some more attractive prospect offers itself, remaining forever open; such 'gymnastic experimentation' in the practical sphere may be regarded, in fact, as the analogue of sophistry in the theoretical. For, whatever the variations, life is still envisaged in terms of possibilities that may be contemplated or savoured, not of projects to be realized or ideals to be furthered.

Such attitudes are held to be symptomatic of something which the judge believes to be endemic to the aesthetic point of view, revealing its ultimate inadequacy. As he puts it, the aestheticist 'expects everything from without'; his approach to the world is basically a passive one, in that his satisfaction is finally subject to conditions whose presence or fulfilment is independent of his will. This submission to the contingent, the 'accidental', to what occurs in the course of events, may take a variety of shapes. Sometimes it is reliance upon 'external' factors, like possessions or power or even the prized affection of another human being; but it may also involve ones that are intrinsic to the individual himself, like health or physical beauty. The point is that, in all instances of this kind, the person is placed at the mercy of circumstances, of 'what may be or may not be'; his mode of life is tied to things that are necessarily uncertain or perishable, and no volition on his part can ever guarantee their attainment or preservation, or even his continued enjoyment of them if he has them. If they fail him – and that will in the end be a matter of chance – it may seem to him that the point of his existence has gone; he will feel, temporarily at least, that he has been deprived of what makes life worth living. As Kierkegaard expressed it elsewhere, in such a view the self is 'a dative, like the "me" of a child its concepts are: good luck, bad luck, fate' (SD 51). Hence it is the mark of the aesthetic individual that he does not seek to impose a coherent pattern on his life, having its source in some unitary notion of himself and of what he should be, but rather allows 'what happens' to act upon him and to govern his behaviour. Inward reflection can show this to be so, and when it occurs it is liable to produce a pervasive sense of despair in the person concerned; his entire life – in general, and not merely in particular respects – may be seen to rest upon an uncertain basis and thus appear drained of meaning. That, however, leads to a further, extremely important, aspect of the aesthetic outlook, and one about which the judge has much to say.

For it is now claimed that such self-awareness may be repressed or ignored, or that at any rate its true implications may be subtly evaded. Despair about his life and its foundation is, in fact, a necessity if the aesthetic individual is to recognize that a 'higher' form of existence is an absolute requirement; yet it is precisely this crucial step in the direction of the ethical that he is unwilling to take. He remains too deeply rooted in his own mode of life and thought to attempt to liberate himself and seeks instead, by a variety of stratagems, to keep the truth from impinging upon him. This sometimes happens through a person's trying to overcome or obliterate his inner dissatisfaction by various kinds of activity: it may take a 'demonic' form, as in the Faustian case; but it can equally well find expression in the life of a 'respectable' man of affairs, going pertinaciously about his business. There is, however, a more insidious shape which it is apt to assume. For there exists what Kierkegaard once called a 'dialectical interplay of knowledge and will' which can make it hard to tell whether a person is consciously trying to distract himself from a predicament which he realizes (however obscurely) to be his or whether, on the other hand, he has so interpreted his condition as to make it appear to preclude the whole notion of fundamental choice and change. And the second of these possibilities may be actualized.

Hence, by a strange modification of the aesthetic position, a man may come to treat sorrow, not pleasure, as 'the meaning of his life', taking a perverse satisfaction in the thought that this at least is something of which he cannot be deprived. For he may regard it as a state to which he is doomed, fated; what he is and feels, how he stands – these all follow inexorably from the nature of things. Thus he may ascribe his unhappiness to something fixed and unalterable in his character or his environment: he has a 'sad disposition', or he has been treated badly by other people. Alternatively, it can be that he portrays himself under grandiloquent labels that somehow determine his place and destiny in the world: for example, the 'unfortunate individual', the 'tragic hero'. Again, and more generally, he may take refuge in a Romantic *Weltschmerz*, using a tone of disillusioned pessimism and treating questions of practical decision as if they could be of no final significance; whatever a man does he will end up regretting. In all such ideas it is possible to find a spurious tranquillity; one can even take a quiet pride in them. For their eventual issue is 'an out and out fatalism, which always has something seductive about it' (EO ii, 241); by accepting a fatalistic or necessitarian viewpoint, the individual tacitly absolves himself from accountability for his condition as well as from an obligation to do anything about it. It is implied, however, that this is never more than a pretence, a cover, behind which he conceals his unavowed determination to remain at a stage from which he could, if he chose, release himself.

All in all, Kierkegaard's analysis of aestheticism is conducted with a psychological subtlety and an elaborate attention to detail that defy brief summary, and it has been possible here only to pick out some of its leading themes. As I have already indicated, he employed his basic categories in an extremely elastic way. This allowed him to point up unexpected connections between apparently diverse phenomena in a manner that can be genuinely illuminating; even so, there are times when his extended use of them seems to put their determinate significance in jeopardy, and a reader of 'Equilibrium' may be excused if he occasionally wonders if there is anything that could not, with a little ingenuity, be interpreted as 'living aesthetically'. Nor is this the sole problem which it poses. For it is not always clear whether Kierkegaard is speaking of the aesthetic consciousness in quite general terms or whether, on the other hand, he is concerned with some specific manifestation of it that was of particular relevance to his own period and culture. There can, however, be no question that he supposed much of what he said to bear upon contemporary currents of thought and behaviour. At one point, for instance, it is explicitly stated that 'aesthetic melancholy', the failure 'to will deeply and sincerely', is a sickness under which 'all young Germany and France now sighs' (EO ii 193). And there are also discernible parallels between the judge's account of certain typical aesthetic attitudes and Kierkegaard's later strictures, in *The Present Age* and elsewhere, on other tendencies implicit in the prevalent social ethos of his time: absorption in the 'outward', the external; absence of a clear sense of individual identity and responsibility; complacent acquiescence in deterministic myths as opposed to serious practical commitment; a pervasive cult of indifference presenting itself under the guise of sophisticated detachment. Nor, as we shall discover, are these imputations unconnected with his subsequent diagnosis of the contemporary appeal and influence of Hegel's metaphysics.

Nevertheless, it would be wrong to identify Kierkegaard's approach to Hegel at the time of writing *Either/Or* too unreservedly with that manifested in some of his later polemics against the 'system'. Admittedly, and as the title itself implies, the book was partly conceived as a protest against the Hegelian notion that distinct forms of consciousness follow one another in a dialectically necessary sequence, mutually opposed standpoints being successively reconciled at higher stages in the progressive unfolding of universal mind or spirit. In Kierkegaard's eyes, the transition from one mode of existence to another conformed to a wholly different pattern. It could only be achieved through an unconstrained and irreducibly personal choice between alternatives; moreover, the alternatives themselves must be seen as being finally incompatible and not such that they could be ultimately harmonized or 'mediated' in the light of some over-arching theoretical insight. Yet, notwithstanding these considerations, the fact remains that the picture of the ethical sphere which actually emerges from 'Equilibrium' is not altogether free from Hegelian overtones. For one thing, the passage to it from the aesthetic is treated as a progressive spiritual movement. Crises occur in the aesthetic consciousness which at least 'call for' the adoption of a new form of life, even if this is not how the person involved himself undertakes to resolve them; as the judge remarks in terms that have a markedly Hegelian ring, there 'comes a moment in a man's life when his immediacy is, as it were, ripened and the spirit demands a higher form in which it will apprehend itself as spirit' (EO ii 193). Further, we are also told that the ethical does not so much 'annihilate the aesthetical' as 'transfigure' it – a remark that consorts a little awkwardly with what Kierkegaard has to say in general about mediation. But it is in the judge's treatment of the relation between the individual and the universal at the ethical level that one is most conscious of the Hegelian background.

In crucial respects the account provided of the ethical point of view appears to focus uncompromisingly upon the individual. Personality is the 'absolute', is 'its own end and purpose'; in describing the emergence and development of the ethical character, the judge treats as basic the notion of 'choosing oneself', this in turn being closely associated with the ideas of self-knowledge, self-acceptance, self-realization. The ethical subject is portrayed as one who regards himself as a 'goal', a 'task set'. Unlike the aestheticist, who is continually preoccupied with externals, his attention is directed towards his own nature, his substantial reality as a human being with such and such talents, inclinations, and passions, this being something which it constantly lies within his power to order, control, and cultivate. There is thus a sense in which he can be said, consciously and deliberately, to take responsibility for himself; he does not, as the aestheticist is prone to do, treat his personal traits and dispositions as an unalterable fact of nature to which he must tamely submit, but regards them rather as a challenge – his self-knowledge is not 'a mere contemplation' but a 'reflection upon himself which itself is an action' (EO ii 263). Moreover, by such inward understanding and critical self-exploration a man comes

9. The wheel of fortune. The ethical individual is immune to the governance of outside circumstances such as accident and fortune.

to recognize, not only what he empirically is, but what he truly aspires to become; thus the judge refers to an 'ideal self' which is the 'picture in likeness to which he has to form himself'. In other words, the ethical individual's life and behaviour must be thought of as infused and directed by a determinate conception of himself which is securely founded upon a realistic grasp of his own potentialities and which is immune to the vicissitudes of accident and fortune. He is not, as the aestheticist was shown to be, the prey of what happens or befalls, for he has not surrendered himself to the arbitrary governance of outside circumstances and incalculable contingencies.

Nor, from the standpoint he adopts, can success or failure be measured by whether or not his projects in fact find fulfilment in the world. What

Enten — Eller.

Et Livs-Fragment

udgivet

af

Victor Eremita.

Første Deel
indeholdende A.'s Papirer.

Er da Fornuften alene døbt,
ere Libenskaberne Hedninger?
Young.

Kjøbenhavn 1843.

Faaes hos Universitetsboghandler C. A. Reitzel.
Trykt i Bianco Lunos Bogtrykkeri.

10. Frontispiece of Kierkegaard's work *Either/Or*.

finally matters is his total identification of himself with these projects; it is the spirit in which things are done, the energy and sincerity with which they are undertaken and pursued, that are relevant here – not the observable consequences of the actions performed.

There is much in all this that strikes a familiar chord, appearing in some ways as an extension of classical doctrines of self-determination that reach back to the Stoics and beyond. But it also has significant affinities to ideas more recently advanced by Kant. Kant, as we noticed earlier on, had stressed the freedom and independence of the moral consciousness, the individual being subject to requirements that derived from his nature as an autonomous, self-directing being. Moreover, it was central to the Kantian position that estimates of moral worth rested solely upon the quality of the agent's will; it was the intentions from which he acted, what he tried to do, that counted here, and not success or failure in actually accomplishing what was aimed at or envisaged. Both these features seem to be reflected, not to say magnified, by Kierkegaard's own account of the moral point of view. Yet that account – at least as so far presented – may strike the reader as inadequate, if only because it appears to interpret the ethical life in a fashion that pays no attention to its content. For it is arguable that a person who lives such a life must also be understood to acknowledge specific norms and values which he regards as holding for others as well as for himself and which justifiably command general agreement and acceptance. And this, indeed, is a point on which B himself seems anxious to insist. Thus the judge certainly goes out of his way to deny that the 'higher form' embodied in the ethical outlook is something which each person is entitled to interpret according to his private tastes and sentiments: such a conception, savouring of 'experimentalism' and ascribable to some kinds of Romanticism, rightfully belongs to the aesthetic, not the ethical, domain. The fundamental categories of the ethical are 'good and evil' and 'duty', and they are referred to as if they had a meaning necessarily shared by all who used them; with this in mind, it can legitimately be affirmed that the ethical individual 'expresses the universal in his life'. But if that is so, how far is it reconcilable with the uncompromisingly self-orientated theory propounded above? There it seemed to be implied that such a man's values ultimately had their source in himself alone: if, on the other hand, he accepts that there exist socially recognized duties which are binding upon him, is he not committed to renouncing his essential independence, being thereby placed once more in a position of subordination to the outward, the external?

To this apparent dilemma Kant's own doctrine of practical reason might have been invoked as offering a solution. According to that doctrine, the moral subject sought to conform to self-imposed principles that satisfied the test of consistency embodied in the Kantian 'categorical imperative' – namely, that the maxim of his action could be 'willed as a universal law'. Respect for such consistency was intrinsic to the 'rational nature' which was common to all human beings in their capacity as moral agents; hence it could be maintained that, for the ethical individual to express what B refers to as 'his inmost nature', it was sufficient that his actions should be governed by rules that met the requirement in question, the general acceptance of these rules being thereby guaranteed. It is far from clear, however, that the judge wishes to endorse such an austerely formal account, and what is in fact said in 'Equilibrium' points towards an Hegelian rather than a Kantian approach to the problem. Amongst other things, Hegel had criticized the Kantian criterion of morality for being too abstract to offer determinate guidance and for appearing to justify any principle, even the most immoral, provided only that no contradiction was involved in willing its universal adoption. Instead, it should be recognized that moral duties were 'rooted in the soil of civil life'. In other words, it was from the practices and institutions embedded in actual societies that both the content and the authority of moral requirements derived, these practices and institutions constituting an intelligible framework whose rationale the ethical subject could appreciate and in terms of which he could fulfil his potentialities as a free and purposive being.

There need be no conflict here between individual aspirations and the demands of communal existence; as an integral part of the society to which he belonged, the individual experienced the duties and responsibilities it imposed, not in the shape of alien constraints, but rather as giving objective form to values and interests that he inwardly acknowledged to be his own. In this way the claims of individual conscience (which Kant had rightly stressed) and the claims inherent in a socially based conception of the moral life were finally reconciled.

It must be admitted that Hegel's theory rested upon certain questionable assumptions about the rational structure of the kinds of society he envisaged; these were connected with his philosophy of history and raise issues that cannot be entered into at this point. None the less, many of the judge's remarks imply that the ethical as he understood it accorded with the Hegelian notion of *Sittlichkeit* just outlined. He says, for instance, that the self which it is the task of the ethical individual to develop must not be thought of as existing 'in isolation', in the manner envisaged by certain 'mystical' doctrines; he stands in 'reciprocal relations' with his public surroundings and conditions of life, the self he seeks to realize being 'a social, a civic self', not an abstract one that 'fits everywhere and hence nowhere'. The judge speaks, too, as if things such as marriage, having a job or useful occupation, undertaking civil and institutional responsibilities, are all essential from this point of view. It did not, however, follow that the duties that derived therefrom presented themselves to such an individual as external limitations, 'foreign to the personality' and restrictive of freedom. Unlike the aestheticist – the 'accidental man' for whom 'the adventitious plays a prodigious role' – he identified himself with the requirements to which he was subject as an active member of society, his character being permeated with the spirit that informed them. In this sense, the universal was not something 'outside the individual'; on the contrary, he was at one with it, giving it concrete expression in the unconstrained fulfilment of those obligations which he recognized to be specifically his. That, indeed, was 'the secret of conscience' – the individual life was conceived to be 'at the same time the universal, if not immediately, yet according to its possibility' (EO ii 260). Thus the gap between the two, which at first sight threatened to undermine the unity and coherence of the ethical outlook, had apparently been closed.

Yet how comprehensive, in the end, does the position set out in 'Equilibrium' turn out to be? Does it provide the only alternative to the aesthetic mode of existence with which it is compared? More crucially, to what extent can it be said to resolve all the problems that may beset a person in the course of his life? The judge himself seems at times to entertain doubts on the latter score; both here and later in *Stages on Life's Way*, where he makes a characteristic reappearance, it is possible to detect strains and tensions underlying the self-confident surface of his prose. As we have seen, there are passages where he appears to be primarily concerned with the subjective quality, the experienced texture, of the life of one who has committed himself to the moral standpoint; whatever efforts he has made elsewhere to accommodate the universal content of the ethical, the fact remains that in these contexts it is not the applicability of general or publicly shared standards which the judge stresses but rather the ways in which the agent approaches what he does and the depth of conviction, of truth to himself, they involve. And it is hard to detach such concern from an implicit preoccupation with the idea that, in the last resort, each person has to find his own path through a process of inner understanding that does justice to his unique individuality and which may, however paradoxically, ultimately carry him beyond the boundaries of the ethical itself. Troublesome suspicions about the self-sufficiency of the ethical outlook and its basic categories emerge towards the end of the judge's disquisitions in *Either/Or* and the *Stages* alike: in both cases, and particularly in the latter, he acknowledges the extreme difficulties certain 'exceptional' individuals may meet when trying to realize the ethical universal in their lives. There, though, the problems raised are only touched upon in a guarded fashion, with careful reservations and with a noticeable reluctance to arrive at a positive resolution. In *Fear and Trembling*, on the other hand, the doubts to which they give rise are given overt and eloquent expression, and in a setting that explicitly contrasts the claims of ethics with those of religion. The frontier that was hesitantly and somewhat obliquely approached in 'Equilibrium' has here been crossed.

Suspension of the ethical

The pseudonymous author of *Fear and Trembling* – Johannes *de silentio* – disclaims any pretensions to be a philosopher, at least in the fashionable Hegelian sense. Nor, it seems clear, does he purport to be a committed Christian, speaking from the standpoint of religious belief. Even so, what he says is evidently intended to bear upon matters that would have been seen by his intended audience as having a philosophical as well as a religious significance. For, although he himself stands within the ethical, he shows himself to be acutely conscious of the apparent limitations of the sphere to which he belongs; more specifically, he is concerned with its inability to comprehend the phenomenon of faith. And his insistence upon the latter point can, of course, be taken as marking a fundamental divergence from approaches of the type initiated by Kant and Hegel. Both writers had, though in very different ways, sought to assimilate or subordinate the notion of religious faith to other categories of thought – Kant by treating its claims as postulates of practical or moral reason, Hegel by regarding it as prefiguring at a pictorial or imaginative level of consciousness ideas that achieved rational articulation within the framework of his own all-encompassing philosophical theory. In *Fear and Trembling*, by contrast, faith is represented as possessing a wholly independent status: it lies beyond the province of ethical thinking and it resists elucidation in universal or rational terms. This does not mean, however, that it should be viewed as something essentially primitive or unworthy of respect; it is not like 'a childhood disease one may wish to get over as soon as possible'. On the contrary, the book concludes with the observation that it constitutes 'the highest passion of a person'. Moreover, it is implied throughout that only an individual who is himself morally sensitive and mature is in a position to recognize the scale of its mysterious and exacting demands.

Kierkegaard's object was to bring home, in a vivid and compelling manner, the disconcerting character of these demands. By focusing attention on a particular instance and by revealing its salient features, he hoped to throw into sharp relief the significance of a concept to which most of his contemporaries paid lip-service but whose actual import had either been smothered by the comfortable words of clergymen or else spirited away by the rationalizations of philosophers. Nor, in doing so, had he any desire to conceal its practical implications. As he goes out of his way to emphasize, in the instance discussed they will inevitably appear shocking, even scandalous, when contemplated within an exclusively ethical perspective.

It can hardly be denied that the example selected was well chosen for the purposes he had in mind. It is drawn from the biblical account of Abraham, the 'father of faith'. Abraham is called upon by God to kill his son, Isaac, offering him as a sacrifice. Abraham follows this instruction, up to the point of drawing the fatal knife; at the last moment, however, his hand is stayed and a ram is provided for him to sacrifice instead. The whole incident is portrayed as a divinely appointed test or spiritual trial, one that he triumphantly passes.

How should one react to such a story? Its value in Kierkegaard's eyes lay, evidently enough, in its stark portrayal of the nature of the choice that confronted Abraham. He could only fulfil God's command by acting, not merely against his natural inclinations as a loving father, but in defiance of the deeply grounded moral principle that forbids the killing of an innocent person; furthermore, the moral enormity of the action was

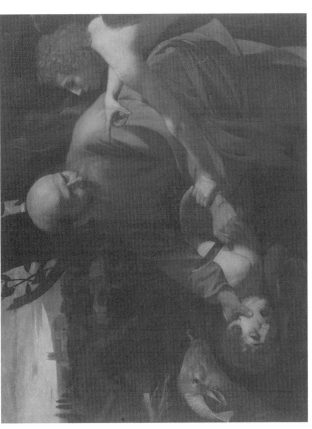

11. Abraham and Isaac, and the demonstration of faith.

compounded by the fact that the person in question was his own son. Thus what he was required to do must have appeared to him, as it does to us, abhorrent on both human and ethical grounds. Yet – as Johannes *de silentio* points out – he is continually praised, from the pulpit and elsewhere, for his grandeur in setting out to accomplish the repulsive task assigned to him. And this raises the question of the extent to which those who indulge in such eulogies have a real grasp of what they are saying. One has merely to imagine how a pastor might address one of his flock who took seriously the possibility of following Abraham's example:

> If the preacher found out about it, he perhaps would go to the man, he would muster all his ecclesiastical dignity and shout, 'You despicable man, you scum of society, what devil has so possessed you that you want to murder your son?'

(FT 28)

He might even take pride in his righteous eloquence. But with what justification? Had he not in his sermons extolled Abraham for the very thing he was now condemning? According to ethics, the answer could only be: yes. Simply stated, 'the ethical expression for what Abraham did is that he meant to murder Isaac'. This was something that had to be faced, clearly and without fudging, by anyone who wished to arrive at a proper comprehension of Abraham's case and of what his action involved. Kierkegaard's pseudonymous author does not claim to understand Abraham himself, in the sense of being able to enter into the content of his life and thought. He does, however, believe that he can lay bare the conditions that make it possible to speak of faith in such a context; he believes, too, that he can thereby illuminate (if only indirectly) the true relationship between the ethical and religious standpoints – a relationship which, in the intellectual climate of his time, has been persistently misconstrued.

One way of approaching what was at issue was to compare Abraham's predicament with that of the moral or 'tragic' hero. An individual of the latter sort also finds himself called upon to do something that is deeply offensive to him, whether on the ground of natural sentiment or because it involves infringing powerful moral constraints, or possibly on account of both. In the case of such a hero, though, the basis upon which he feels bound to act is itself a recognizably ethical one: an example Kierkegaard gives is Agamemnon's decision to sacrifice his daughter Iphigenia for the sake of the state. He is vindicated in his own eyes by the fact that in performing the terrible deed he still 'reposes' within the ethical universal; whatever the pain it causes him, however deep his feelings of personal loss and of compunction, he none the less has the assurance that he is conforming to the requirements of an acknowledged principle or general objective with which he can identify and which takes precedence over all other considerations. Hence, in the hard circumstances confronting him, he can legitimately expect the sympathy and respect of those around him – 'the tragic hero gives up the certain for the even more certain, and the observer's eye views him with confidence' (FT 60). He is at least able to 'rejoice in the security of the universal', knowing that what he does can be defended in terms that all, including even its victims, are in a position to recognize and understand.

Things are quite otherwise with Abraham, the 'knight of faith'. The tragic hero, we are told, still treats the ethical as his 'telos' or goal, even if this entails subordinating particular duties to its attainment. Abraham, on the other hand, has transgressed the ethical altogether, having a higher telos outside it 'in relation to which he suspended it'. And this 'relinquishment of the universal' involves a degree of distress that surpasses any attributable to his moral counterpart. He stands isolated and alone, without the possibility of justifying to others an action which, at the level of rational thought and conduct, must necessarily appear outrageous, indeed absurd. As a particular individual he has placed himself in 'an absolute relation to the absolute'. If his action is justifiable, it can only be by reference to a divine command that is addressed to him alone and whose content is such that he cannot hope to render what he does intelligible by human standards; according to those, he must be deemed either to be mad or else simply hypocritical. Moreover, the very attempt to vindicate himself in humanly understandable terms would be tantamount to seeking to evade the conditions of the task assigned to him, a task that presupposes an absolute duty to God which transcends the domain of ethical discourse and which must be fulfilled in the face of all temptations to the contrary. It was by resisting these temptations – moral as well as natural – that Abraham withstood the trial to which his faith was subjected. He was prepared, in other words, to follow through to the end the frightening consequences of his paradoxical commitment; therein lay his true claim to the 'greatness' which is often, but largely unthinkingly, accorded him.

There is an undeniable poignancy about Kierkegaard's depiction of the plight of those who pursue in anguish their undisclosed missions and who in doing so 'walk without meeting one single traveller'. What he writes has the sharp flavour of personal experience and suggests that he partly had in mind his own sense of distraught isolation at the time of his broken engagement; it may also evoke the vertiginous feelings induced by practical dilemmas that seem to elude the grasp of general categories and where a person can come to view compliance with established norms as threatening his integrity as an individual. But, however impressive psychologically, such considerations do nothing in themselves to validate his central thesis. For this concerns the possibility of a 'teleological' suspension of the ethical by the religious, and it is one that has – perhaps not unnaturally – run into a good deal of criticism. Amongst other things, the contention that in certain circumstances all ethical requirements may be set aside has been stigmatized as amounting to the advocacy of a 'moral nihilism' which no rhetorical appeals of the kind he provides can conceivably excuse, let alone justify. To invoke beliefs which apparently entail an acquiescence in 'the absurd' in order to legitimize morally abhorrent deeds is scarcely to the purpose; if anything, its sole effect must be to undermine confidence in all our valuations, since it permits the rejection of even those about which we feel most assured. It may, of course, be replied that Abraham, considered as a 'knight of faith', was not acting *in vacuo* and without warrant: he was carrying out what he took to be the will of God. But what were the grounds for that assurance? As Kant drily noted, when discussing the very example Kierkegaard later took as his model, 'it is at least possible that in this instance a mistake has prevailed'. Where a supposedly divine command conflicts with a moral judgement that impresses us as being intrinsically certain, we have the clear option of refusing to ascribe it to God. And in Kant's view – as presented in his *Religion within the Limits of Reason Alone* – that was the option which, in a case of the sort described, a 'conscientious' individual would naturally and correctly choose.

From what Kierkegaard says it would appear that there is a sense in which he had no wish to dissent from this. In so far as such an individual is defined as one who takes his stand upon ethics alone, moral judgements that seem self-evident to human reason must certainly, indeed necessarily, be decisive in his eyes. From the position in question the whole of human existence is seen as a 'perfect self-contained sphere' which ethics fills and completes, God himself being thereby reduced to 'an invisible vanishing point'. Here people may, to be sure, use religious language, speaking of the duty to love and obey the Deity; but in their employment of such expressions what they really mean comes down to no more than a truism. As it is put in one place:

> If in this connection I . . . say that it is my duty to love God, I am actually pronouncing only a tautology, inasmuch as 'God' in a totally abstract sense is here understood as the divine – that is, the universal, that is, duty.

> (FT 68)

In the discussion that follows this passage, Kierkegaard reverts to the point on which much of his essay can be said to turn. It was one thing to accord supremacy to the ethical; it was quite another to maintain that the religious could be reduced to this, its essential content being expressible in terms wholly acceptable to finite reason. From a religious point of view, ethics never possesses more than a 'relative' status; the denial that from that standpoint it could be envisaged as ultimate or supreme was something which his treatment of the Abraham story was expressly designed to bring into sharp focus. But to insist that it only had relative validity was not to assert that it had no validity at all: it did not follow from his account of the story that moral requirements were devoid of all foundation or that they could in a general way be dispensed with. What he did wish to argue was that within a religious perspective they took on an altered aspect, received a 'completely different expression'. And by this he seems partly to have meant that the obligation to conform to them finally rests upon a prior commitment to God, where the latter is conceived to be an infinite or absolute 'other' that transcends human reason and understanding: 'the single individual . . . determines his relation to the universal by his relation to the absolute, not his relation to the absolute by his relation to the universal' (FT 70).

In one sense it is possible to regard *Fear and Trembling* as simply making a point about the religious consciousness which contemporary theorists, and above all those of an Hegelian persuasion, chose to distort or else to reason away. Whatever they might protest to the contrary, on their view of the matter to act as Abraham did was to stand condemned. None the less, faith as he understood it and exemplified it in his life is presupposed by the religious consciousness, and any attempt to present the 'inner truth' of religion in a fashion that eliminates or emasculates what such faith involves must necessarily be misconceived. But the incapacity of current thought to come to terms with the religious outlook was by no means the sole object of Kierkegaard's concern; here, as in his other 'aesthetic' books, what he wrote was not intended to be a mere exercise in academic criticism. By throwing into the strongest relief the contrast between the standpoint of faith and one that made ethics supreme, he also sought to silhouette the limitations of the latter – limitations that emerged when proper account was taken of vital aspects of personal experience which were resistant to its sway and with which it seemed powerless to deal. As we have noticed, intimations of these appeared at certain moments in the judge's presentation of the ethical position in *Either/Or* and *Stages on Life's Way*. There it was suggested that an individual may believe himself to be subject to the demands of a unique calling which cannot be accommodated within the framework of socially determined duties or universally accepted principles of conduct; yet the status of such an awareness must inevitably be problematic, and the judge shows no inclination to play down the consequences incurred by trying to follow it:

> He must comprehend that no one can understand him, and must have the constancy to put up with it that human language has for him naught but curses and the human heart has for his sufferings only the one feeling that he is guilty.
>
> (SLW 175)

At the level of religious faith, which is the theme of *Fear and Trembling*, the significance of these intimations becomes at last fully manifest. While the importance of moral requirements is not as such denied, the absolute sovereignty of the ethical can no longer be assumed; rather, it is transcended by a perspective in which the self-sufficiency of morality, regarded as a socially established and universally acknowledged institution, is explicitly challenged. The notion that a person might be conscious of an 'exceptional' mission, to be fulfilled at whatever cost and in the face of ostensibly overwhelming objections, was not something that could be simply passed over or shrugged off, nor could it be relegated to 'the rather commonplace company of feelings, moods, idiosyncrasies, *vapeurs*, etc.' (FT 69). Abraham's conception of his assignment belied all this: in seeking to accomplish it he was not only prepared to resist the dictates of ordinary morality; he further believed – against every rational expectation – that he would in some fashion 'receive back' the son he had been commanded to sacrifice. To complain that what he did was contrary to reason, that he ran a terrible risk and might be making a mistake, was in a way true enough; it merely served, however, to underline the distinctive character of the standpoint he occupied. Faith in the sense here in question lay outside the aegis of human standards of rationality, and the transition to what it involved was not susceptible to justification in those terms. On the contrary, it demanded a radical venture or 'leap', a spiritual movement requiring a commitment to something that was objectively uncertain and in the last analysis paradoxical.

In order to grasp the underlying tenor of such pronouncements regarding the true import of religious faith, it is necessary to turn to what Kierkegaard referred to as his 'philosophical works'. These will be the subject of the next chapter. But before taking leave of the 'aesthetic' literature, we must revert briefly to an issue alluded to at the close of the previous chapter.

That, it will be remembered, concerned Kierkegaard's later contention that his imaginative presentation of different modes of existence had been essentially directed towards leading his readers out of the illusion that they were Christians. As he put it in the *Point of View*, they lived in 'aesthetic, or, at the most, aesthetic-ethical categories' and hence were unable to appreciate the depth of the deception, or self-deception, in which they were immersed: by approaching such persons through their own characteristic ways of thinking and by appearing in the first instance to 'go along' with these, it might be possible to cause them to see for themselves the extent and the sources of their pervasive misunderstandings. Yet, whatever attractions this view of his overall intent held for Kierkegaard himself when he looked back on his career as an author, it may none the less strike one as being somewhat strained when the full content and range of the writings in question are taken into account. It is not merely that they often give the strong impression of having been to a considerable degree motivated by autobiographical preoccupations, including a compulsive fascination with the course taken by his abortive love-affair. It would also appear that, at least so far as the aesthetic outlook is concerned, the 'illusions' allegedly fostered are related to fatalistic or collectivist myths about the human condition rather than to anything specifically connected with the false consciousness ascribed to contemporary 'Christendom'. If there is supposed to be an association with the latter it seems at best to be an indirect one. It may be, though, that Kierkegaard meant no more than that an aesthetically attuned individual is liable to view Christianity as something which – along with everything else – demands no serious commitment on his part; it is simply 'interesting', a subject that invites detached contemplation as opposed to decisive action and participation. In any event, his retrospective claim may impress us as being more obviously applicable to what he had to say, in *Fear and Trembling*, about the invasion of the religious standpoint by categories of thought that belonged to the ethical rather than to the aesthetic sphere. Here it is easier to see what he might have had in mind.

Chapter 5
Truth and subjectivity

Kierkegaard's portrayal of distinguishable modes of life and experience
prepared the way for the two major works upon which his reputation as
a religious thinker chiefly rests: the brief and relatively condensed
Philosophical Fragments and the lengthy, polemical, and often very
repetitive *Concluding Unscientific Postscript*. Like their predecessors, they
were both published under a pseudonym – in the present instance that
of Johannes Climacus (John the Climber) – but with the difference that
here Kierkegaard's name also appeared, he being referred to as their
'editor'. Whatever precise significance should be attached to the
change, it is at least reasonable to assume that in this case the views
expressed were intended to be understood as being essentially his own:
his aim was to exhibit, as explicitly and forcefully as possible, the true
significance of the 'misunderstanding between speculative philosophy
and Christianity' which he believed to be endemic to the intellectual
outlook of his age. The aesthetic writings might have helped to indicate,
albeit indirectly and allusively, how it was that various psychological and
social attitudes had contributed to the growth of this
misunderstanding; there remained, however, the central task of
delineating its fundamental character and of eliciting its
presuppositions. Such was the task to which he now addressed himself,
and in doing so he chose as his principal targets Hegel and those who
had been influenced by him. None the less, and despite his intense
preoccupation with current tendencies, he regarded his diagnosis of

what was involved as being of more than merely contemporary relevance. It had wider implications; *au fond*, the questions at issue concerned the very nature of religious faith and its relation to the resources of human thought and rationality. The manner in which some of these questions arose at the level of practical choice had already been indicated in *Fear and Trembling*. In the *Fragments* and the *Postscript* they were to reappear, but now transposed to a context where more was at stake than the scope of ethics and the limits of moral reasoning, and where faith in the specifically Christian sense, rather than that ascribed to Abraham, became the prime object of attention.

Behind both books one can in fact discern the influence of two 18th-century authors who, in Kierkegaard's eyes, had already brought certain crucial aspects of Christian belief into sharp focus. One of these was J. G. Hamann (1730–88), a maverick thinker whose writings Kierkegaard had first encountered in his student days and whose uncompromising attacks on rationalism – both in theology and elsewhere – seem to have struck him with the force of a revelation. The other was G. E. Lessing (1729–81), whose seminal essay *On the Proof of the Spirit and of Power* he appears to have come across some years later through reading Strauss's *The Christian Faith*. About the significance of Hamann's impact there will be something to say in due course. The views expressed in Lessing's essay, on the other hand, are of more immediate concern, since they were explicitly referred to by Kierkegaard as constituting a common point of departure for the *Fragments* and the *Postscript* alike.

The basic issue discussed by Lessing concerned the status of Christianity as an historically orientated religion. How was it possible to ground its central claims, including the proposition that Christ was the son of God, upon no more than certain putatively historical facts? It was not just that the latter presumably stood in need of the kind of evidential ratification normally required in historical enquiry. Even if they were allowed to have strong empirical support, this would still not amount to assigning them more than a high probability; historical statements, however well attested, were necessarily incapable of achieving the degree of certitude ascribable to first-hand or eye-witness reports of present experience. Nor was this the end of the difficulties that arose. For there remained the further problem of how assertions regarding particular matters of historical fact could be adduced to justify the acceptance of propositions of a dogmatically transcendent character. What, in other words, legitimized the transition from a set of ostensibly empirical claims to another set that belonged to an entirely different category? As Lessing put it:

> If on historical grounds I have no objection to the statement that Christ raised to life a dead man; must I therefore accept it as true that God has a Son who is of the same essence as himself? What is the connection between my inability to raise any significant objection to the evidence of the former and my obligation to believe something against which my reason rebels?

Faced by such questions, Lessing spoke in a well-known passage of there being an 'ugly, broad ditch which I cannot get across, however often and however earnestly I have tried to make the leap'. Although he did not make his own position unambiguously clear, he seems instead to have endorsed a 'demythologized' conception of the religious message which treated it as embodying predominantly ethical truths that could be inwardly apprehended by reason alone. Such truths, being universal and timelessly valid, could not conceivably be founded upon, or derived from, ones whose status was purely contingent; thus, if historical factors were taken to be relevant here, it could only be as illustrating and giving temporal expression to an independently identifiable moral content – in the sense favoured by Lessing, religion was not true because 'evangelists and apostles' taught it, but they taught it because it was true. Or, as he put it elsewhere, historical revelation 'gives nothing to the human race which human reason could not arrive at on its own'.

72

Whatever conclusions Lessing might himself have drawn, for Kierkegaard his cardinal merit lay in his having accurately grasped the nature of the dilemma that confronted him. The dogmatic tenets of Christian orthodoxy were not conformable to reason, nor was it possible to validate them through merely historical considerations that were in any case intrinsically problematic. Hence there was a need to choose between, on the one hand, taking a 'qualitative' or categorical leap of the kind that had defeated Lessing himself and, on the other, discarding the tenets in question in favour of some alternative which was acceptable from the standpoint of human understanding and rationality: no middle path stood open. This, indeed, is the dominant theme underlying Kierkegaard's *Fragments*, and variations on it continue to recur throughout his subsequent *Postscript*: it was necessary above all to counter the contention that Christianity represented a doctrine which could be objectively justified, whether in terms of speculative thought or by an appeal to historical knowledge. In exploring that theme, however, he took up and developed its implications in a fashion very much his own.

Reason and faith

Despite its brevity, *Philosophical Fragments* is not an easy book to read; the mode of exposition is somewhat eccentric and the line of thought undergoes sudden breaks and transitions which at times induce a certain bewilderment. Nevertheless, it appears at the start that the main focus is to be upon two distinct approaches to the problem of how the truth can be learned. Although raised initially in what seems to be a wholly general way, it quickly becomes clear that it is with the problem of the status and acquisition of religious truth that the work is principally concerned.

Kierkegaard begins by setting against one another two radically opposed answers to his original question. The first he associates with Plato and his doctrine of 'recollection'. In Plato's *Meno* a puzzle is posed as to how we can ever hope to acquire knowledge at all; for if the truth is already known it cannot be sought, while if it is not known how can it be recognized as being the truth when it is encountered or presented? On either alternative learning appears to be conceptually impossible. Plato – whose primary concern, incidentally, was with such 'timeless' truths as those of mathematics – claimed that the solution lay in realizing that learning was a matter of the subject's becoming aware of what was present, though dormant, in his own mind, and that the teacher's function consisted in reminding him of what he implicitly possessed; it was a matter of tapping or unlocking knowledge that was in some sense already there. 'The truth' – in Kierkegaard's words – 'is not introduced into the individual from without, but was within him.' It followed from such a theory that the role of the teacher could never be more than a purely 'accidental' one, since the very same result might have been brought about by some quite different person or in some quite different circumstances, and Kierkegaard in effect treats this position as being representative of a pervasive rationalism that was widely shared amongst speculative philosophers, not least by the Idealists of his own time. It is indeed true that Hegel himself had more than once suggested that the Platonic notion of knowledge as recollection (*Erinnerung*) bore some analogies to his own view that reality as a whole was generated by principles latent within our thinking processes, its fundamental character being such that it could be elicited by philosophical reflection upon these. But in any event, and however diverse the forms in which it manifested itself, Kierkegaard held that what united theorists of the kind he had in mind was an unquestioned belief in human reason as the sole source of ultimate or essential truth.

The alternative standpoint, which on Kierkegaard's interpretation turns out to be that of Christianity, rests upon presuppositions totally at variance with those he has ascribed, with a certain insouciance, to thinkers in the Platonic tradition. The basic contentions of the latter are in this case not so much rejected as reversed.

74

Thus according to the contrasting position the individual is not accredited with an implicit possession of ultimate truth which can be activated by some sort of philosophical 'midwifery'. On the contrary, he is portrayed as being externally related to something which transcends him and to which he is a stranger; he must 'be characterised as beyond the pale of the Truth, not approaching it like a proselyte, but departing from it' (PF 16). The suggestion here – one to which Kierkegaard constantly adverts – is that the individual's being so estranged is not a mere accident or temporary disability; rather, it is a state of affairs for which he himself is fundamentally responsible and which, as such, may be described as one of 'sin' – he is not only 'outside the Truth' but 'polemic' in his attitude towards it. Two things are said to follow from this. First, truth in the sense in question, since it is not possessed by the individual, can only be brought to him from the outside: secondly, he himself will have to be inwardly changed if he is to be in a position to recognize it, as otherwise his own corruption and self-imposed blindness will prevent him from doing so. But a teacher who is capable both of bringing the truth to the learner and of providing him with the condition that is requisite if he is to grasp it cannot be another human being: it can only be God.

> One who gives the learner not only the Truth, but also the condition for understanding it, is more than teacher . . . ; if it is to be done, it must be done by the God himself.
>
> (PF 18)

At the same time, however, the truth must not be transmitted in a manner that would overawe the learner or dazzle him into submission, for then he would not be accepting it willingly and in a way that allows for freedom of choice, but from some extraneous motive like fear. Instead it must be presented as coming from an equal with whom he can communicate on level terms, and this means that the God has to appear to him in human form. We are confronted, in other words, with the Christian conception of the incarnation.

Such a conception is paradoxical. Indeed, according to Kierkegaard, it represents what he calls the 'Absolute Paradox'. For it requires us to believe that there is a moment at which the eternal enters the temporal sphere, taking on the limitations of finite existence, and this seems to involve a manifest impossibility, something that cannot be accommodated within the bounds of human thought and comprehension. Hence it will necessarily be 'offensive' in the eyes of reason; the latter will 'find it impossible to conceive it, could not of itself have discovered it, and when it hears it announced will not be able to understand it' (PF 59). Nevertheless, it constitutes the proper object of faith, and that is only to confirm the point that Lessing had clearly seen: faith and reason cannot be reconciled and either the one or the other must give way. To remain at the level of the rational is to be committed to rejecting the Paradox; from this point of view it is an 'absurdity'. Faith, on the other hand, reveals itself when the categories of reason are set aside and the individual makes the 'leap' which acknowledging the special character of the teacher demands. Kierkegaard insists, however, that the leap in question cannot be taken without the teacher's assistance. It presupposes what he has termed the 'condition', since unless the learner's nature has been transformed through an act of divine grace he will be unable to perform it; to suppose otherwise would be to assume, what has expressly been denied, that he can become aware of the truth by virtue of his corrupted powers alone. There can thus be said to be two paradoxical 'moments' – the moment of the incarnation and the moment of faith – the second of which is the correlate of the first and both of which must be deemed 'miraculous':

> But in that case is not Faith as paradoxical as the Paradox? Precisely so; how else could it have the Paradox for its object, and be happy in its relation to the Paradox? Faith is itself a miracle, and all that holds true of the Paradox also holds true of Faith.

(PF 81)

In contemplating Kierkegaard's account of the Christian position we should remember that – ostensibly at least – his purpose in the present context was not to defend or justify it but rather to draw attention to what it involved. And from what has been said it will be obvious that, far from playing down the intellectual difficulties it might be felt to raise, he went out of his way to accentuate them; he wanted to highlight, not to obscure, its distance from our natural modes of thought, stressing the obstacles the latter inevitably encountered when they came into contact with what lay beyond their scope. Yet at the same time he did not wish to deny that the human intellect had an inveterate tendency to seek to surmount the limits that bounded it, in a vain effort to absorb within its own categories or principles of understanding matters that necessarily eluded their grasp. Hence he maintained that, in compliance with this tendency, philosophers and theologians were frequently tempted to try to assimilate the transcendent claims of the Christian religion to familiar or well-entrenched conceptions of knowledge: 'why', he asks ironically at one point, 'do we have our philosophers, if not to make supernatural things trivial and commonplace?' (PF 66). One form this project took was that of attempting to prove the existence of God by invoking exclusively rational considerations of the sort he associated in the first instance with the Platonic standpoint. Another, and markedly different, approach consisted, not in seeking to derive religious conclusions from resources supplied by pure reason, but in appealing instead to evidential support of the kind provided by history. In either case, however, only failure could result, as Kierkegaard sets out to show.

His objections to the former line of argument, though important, largely echo ones that had previously been brought by Kant. Kant contended (as Hume had done before him) that reason, considered by itself and independently of all experience, was confined to operating with ideas or concepts alone; as such, it was powerless on its own account to demonstrate the existence of anything. Thus attempts to establish that God exists by reference simply to the concept of God, as in the case of the so-called 'ontological proof', are broken-backed. It is impossible to derive from the bare notion of a perfect being the substantial assertion that such a being exists: as Kierkegaard remarks, by this means 'I do not prove . . . an existence, but merely develop the content of a conception' (PF 49); the conceptual or ideal 'essence of God' must be clearly distinguished from his 'factual being', and the latter is the point here at issue. Even if, as might at first sight appear plausible, I try instead to infer his existence from alleged manifestations of divine workmanship in the order of nature, nothing of consequence follows; the manifestations referred to presuppose an 'ideal interpretation' which I have already tacitly put upon the facts and hence afford no independent justification for the desired conclusion.

Thus briefly surveyed, sceptical objections to the course traditionally pursued by natural theology are felt by Kierkegaard to be irresistible. The exercise of reason in the requisite sense deals solely with conceptual or tautological truths, any appearance to the contrary being due to the presence of certain crucial assumptions covertly made in advance; it is therefore quite useless for the task assigned to it. What, though, of the alternative offered by turning from such abstract considerations to the positive claims of revelation? May there still not be sound reasons for accepting these, this time on specifically historical grounds? Amongst other things, such an approach – unlike the first – has the advantage of doing justice to an aspect of Christianity upon which Kierkegaard himself was concerned to insist, namely, the central emphasis placed on the occurrence and implications of a unique historical event. So it is not surprising to find him devoting an extended discussion to the status of historical enquiry and its relation to faith.

Although the account Kierkegaard provides is a notoriously contorted one, the following points may be said to emerge. In the first place, he stresses the irreducibly contingent or non-necessary character of historical occurrence and change; theorists who, like Hegel, illicitly sought to fuse historical with logical or metaphysical categories, thereby treating the realm of history as the embodiment of necessary conceptual relationships, were radically mistaken. Secondly, he implies that recognition of this feature has important consequences from an epistemological point of view. Propositions about the human past, being contingent and factual, are necessarily devoid of the certitude that belongs to conceptually demonstrable truths of reason. But neither do they possess the certainty which can justifiably be ascribed to propositions that are confined to reporting our immediate experience. This, indeed, holds even of ordinary observational claims which purport to go beyond the indubitable data of sensation – one has only (Kierkegaard suggests) to consider well-worn examples of perceptual illusion to realize that the contemporary spectator of an event may be mistaken about the actual character of what he is witnessing. In any case, so far as historical statements are concerned, there is a manifest gap between what they assert and the evidence for them, a gap that effectively deprives them of logical guarantee as to their truth. What, then, is it to accept them? Kierkegaard says that the appropriate category to apply here is that of *belief*, where that should be understood as involving an 'expression of will' rather than a rational inference; what we have to do with is 'not so much a conclusion as a resolution', a voluntary act that 'excludes doubt'. So conceived, belief inevitably runs the risk of committing itself to what is untrue and must be distinguished from knowledge in the strict sense. None the less, it appears from what he writes elsewhere that he thinks it legitimate to ascribe varying degrees of probability to propositions about empirical matters of fact, including historical ones; thus we can speak (as he himself does in the *Postscript*) of our at least having 'approximation-knowledge' of them. And this brings us to his third, and central, point.

It is vital to differentiate between belief in the 'direct or ordinary sense' – the sense relevant to standard historical claims – and belief, or faith, in the 'eminent sense' which relates to the 'paradoxical' historical claim of Christianity. Although belief of the former kind cannot be rationally certified, it is constitutive of our normal attitudes to the world and represents a wholly natural dimension of human consciousness. Belief of the second type, on the other hand, requires us to accept something which – as was seen earlier – is offensive to reason and baffles the understanding. It follows that those who suppose that the object of Christian faith can somehow be justified, or at any rate rendered probable, by appealing to the accredited procedures of history betray a fundamental misapprehension of its nature. We are not dealing here with some straightforward or run-of-the-mill historical hypothesis, to be deemed more or less likely according to the available documentary evidence: 'this historical fact which is the content of our hypothesis has a peculiar character, since it is not an ordinary historical fact, but a fact based on a self-contradiction' (PF 108). We are assuming, that is to say, that the 'eternal' or timeless has come into existence in time, and to talk of probability in such a connection is evidently out of place. According to Kierkegaard, moreover, it is culpably misguided: 'to make such an assertion about Faith is to slander it.' Apart from anything else, it may be taken to imply that the belief in question was better authenticated for those who actually witnessed the events recorded in the Gospels than it could ever be for members of subsequent generations. But this is a supposition which he goes to great lengths to deny. The acceptance of something conceived to be intrinsically paradoxical cannot be subject to the vagaries of temporal situation or circumstance. It must have been just as possible for a contemporary witness to fail to perceive the import of the incarnation simply on the basis of what he saw or heard as it is for successors who have only testimony to go on; either way, what is presented can never be more than an 'occasion' for faith.

> There is no disciple at second hand. The first and the last are essentially on the same plane, only that a later generation finds its occasion in the testimony of a contemporary generation, while the contemporary generation finds this occasion in its own immediate contemporaneity.
>
> (PF 131)

Religiously speaking, neither has the edge over the other. In every case faith demands, not just a leap, but a leap into the rationally unthinkable which presupposes divine assistance. This is sufficient to put out of court any suggested comparison between different temporal vantage-points. Faith, as Kierkegaard understands it, is not a matter of superior evidence or conditions of observation; its possibility depends, as has been seen, on a miracle.

Kierkegaard's repeated references to the miraculous character of religious faith – rendering it totally incommensurable with all accepted forms of human cognition – are reminiscent of the famous passage in Hume's *Enquiry Concerning Human Understanding* to which I briefly referred in chapter 2. As some recent writers have pointed out, there are in fact discernible parallels of a general kind between Hume's epistemological position and the view of secular knowledge and belief implicit in the *Fragments*. Thus both tend to restrict the attribution of cognitive certainty to necessary truths of reason and to propositions reporting immediate sensory data: likewise, both again imply that causal inferences concerning matters of empirical fact are lacking in rational, in the sense of demonstrative, justification. It is true that, whereas Hume sought to account for such inferences psychologically in terms of customary or habitual expectations deriving from our past experience of regularities, Kierkegaard by contrast – and rather oddly – speaks of their being the expression of volitions; even here, however, the contrast appears less marked if one bears in mind the particular fashion in which he goes on to develop his distinction between 'ordinary' and 'eminent' senses of belief. And these parallels take on an added and more specific significance in the present context. For Hume had argued in the *Enquiry*, not only that there were objections in principle to the project of a rationally based natural theology, but that attempts to establish religious claims instead by appealing to scriptural testimony regarding allegedly supernatural occurrences could never carry conviction in the face of the overwhelming mass of our ordinary experience of the world. Hence in the last paragraph of his section on miracles he concluded that 'the *Christian Religion* not only was at first attended with miracles, but even at this day cannot be believed by any reasonable person without one'. He went on:

Mere reason is insufficient to convince us of its veracity: And whoever is moved by *Faith* to assent to it, is conscious of a continued miracle in his own person, which subverts all the principles of his understanding, and gives him a determination to believe what is most contrary to custom and experience.

Despite obvious divergences of emphasis and tone, the overall similarity between the tenor of Hume's conclusion and that of Kierkegaard's own account of faith is sufficiently close to arouse the suspicion that it cannot have been entirely fortuitous. And this suspicion seems to be well founded. In an early journal entry Kierkegaard recorded how, when reading Hamann, he had come across a specific reference to the passage quoted above: 'Hume', Hamann remarked, 'may have said this with a scornful and critical air, yet all the same, this is orthodoxy and a witness to the truth from the mouth of an enemy and persecutor – all his doubts are proofs of his proposition.' What appears especially to have impressed Kierkegaard – here as elsewhere in Hamann's anti-intellectualist writings – was the latter's rejection of *a priori* theorizing as a source of genuine discovery and illumination and the stress he had laid instead upon *Glaube* or faith, this being an unmediated and divinely inspired gift of spiritual vision whose insights were fatally obscured by the logical cobwebs spun by natural theologians and speculative metaphysicians alike. Hume's cardinal merit, in Hamann's opinion, lay in his having effectively undermined all attempts to substantiate in rational or commonsensical terms claims which were not susceptible to demonstration by argument and which did not fall within the province of the abstract or generalizing understanding: though himself an unbelieving ironist, he thus emerged – however unwittingly – as an ally of the very religion he ostensibly derided. As we have noticed, Kierkegaard followed his German predecessor in acknowledging fully the force of the sceptic's objections; if the tenets of Christian belief were subjected to assessments of the kind attributable to Hume's 'reasonable person' they must inevitably seem to be, not merely unwarranted, but absurd. And (again like Hamann) he viewed these objections as performing the salutary service of removing perennial misconceptions concerning the actual character of such belief, thereby throwing into sharp relief its essential import when seen within a perspective appropriate to what was at issue. Those who wished to justify it in a manner that conformed to the requirements of ordinary thought and experience were the victims of a profound misunderstanding – one, moreover, that could be deemed culpable in so far as it amounted to an evasion of what was crucially at stake. As Hamann had observed, 'lies and romances must be probable, hypotheses and fables; but not the truth and fundamental doctrine of our faith': the latter constituted 'a sphere all by itself', and every effort to establish its validity by invoking the resources of objective knowledge and enquiry involved a 'confusion of the categories' as well as representing a 'temptation of the spirit'. In the light of such considerations, Lessing's own insistence upon the leap demanded by a commitment to the transcendent claims of Christianity assumed for Kierkegaard an amplified and compelling meaning, with momentous consequences so far as the individual was concerned.

What he took those consequences to be becomes apparent in the *Concluding Unscientific Postscript*. There, however, they are presented in a setting which gives prominence not so much to traditional attempts to provide Christian belief with a rational backing as to the one that had recently found favour amongst followers of the 'latest philosophy'. Oblique allusions to Hegelian themes can undoubtedly be detected in the *Fragments*; none the less, Kierkegaard was aware of the need to distinguish between Hegel's particular mode of subjecting the religious consciousness to the categories of reason and previous efforts to do so of a kind which it was intended to supersede. Accordingly, in the *Postscript* we find him undertaking a sustained and comprehensive critique which was specifically addressed to the implications of the Hegelian theory.

Errors of Hegelianism

Given the general and in some ways misleadingly stark division drawn at the start of the *Fragments*, it is not hard to see why Hegel's approach to religion should have engaged Kierkegaard's especial attention. For, whatever might be the case with other positions, Hegel's idealism reflected in a strikingly uncompromising form the conviction that reality could be rendered wholly transparent to human reason. As such, it was not content with trying to offer theoretical support to accepted Christian dogmas; it purported to provide a correct interpretation of their real, if latent, content. In doing so, however, it appeared – at least in Kierkegaard's eyes – to have in effect transformed them, divesting them of their essential character and treating their distinctive features as dispensable manifestations of an immature outlook which it was the destiny of philosophy finally to transcend. In his own words:

> For a man to prefer paganism to Christianity is by no means confusing, but to discover paganism as a highest development within Christianity is to work injustice both to paganism and to Christianity ... The speculative movement which plumes itself on having completely understood Christianity, and explains itself at the same time as the highest development within Christianity, has strangely enough made the discovery that there is no 'beyond'. The notions of a future life, of another world, and similar ideas are described as arising out of the dialectical limitations of the finite understanding.
>
> (CUP 323)

To be sure, this had not prevented Hegelians from often employing religious language in formulating their views; Kierkegaard's contention that 'the entire Christian terminology has been appropriated by speculative thought to its own purposes' may be an exaggeration but it is not without foundation. Thus Hegel himself frequently referred to God when describing the character and development of absolute spirit, even going so far as to call his own philosophy a 'theodicy': he was ready, too, to incorporate within his system the historical dimension of Christianity, treating notions like that of the incarnation as expressing the relation of men to a cosmic process in which they necessarily participated as finite, self-conscious beings. Yet he can hardly be said to have been a theist in any orthodox sense, Christian or otherwise. As we saw earlier, Hegelian *Geist* was not regarded as realizing itself independently of mankind, nor was ultimate truth something imparted to us 'from outside', through acts of divine grace. The emphatic denial of a supersensible 'beyond' – whether that was envisaged pictorially or whether it was abstractly conceived as a Kantian postulate or 'idea' – was intrinsic to the fundamental notion of a self-determining and self-differentiating spiritual principle which fulfilled itself in the *human* world and which could only come to an awareness of itself through the consciousness of creatures like ourselves. As Hegel himself put it in the third part of his *Encyclopaedia*, God is only God in so far as he knows himself and he can only know himself through man.

It was, however, one thing to insist that – despite its pretensions – Hegel's interpretation of religion radically distorted the actual significance of the Christian message; it was another to evaluate the philosophy from which that interpretation derived and to which it owed its credentials. Kierkegaard wished to demonstrate that the Hegelian metaphysic, considered on its own and judged in terms of its declared ambition to afford a comprehensive account of reality, was in point of fact flawed, and irreparably so. For the weakness of the overall structure lay in its very foundations.

In propounding his criticisms, Kierkegaard drew partly upon ones that had already been levelled against Hegel both by Feuerbach and by Adolf Trendelenburg (1802–72), a shrewd Aristotelian scholar and logician whom he much admired. As he himself presents them, they take the form of an ironic and often diffuse commentary on certain key speculative assumptions rather than of a step-by-step examination of

12. Ludwig Andreas Feuerbach (1804–1872).

Hegel's particular arguments and inferences; those looking for an ordered set of neatly marshalled objections will not find it here. Nevertheless, there is a sense in which the absence of such detailed analyses was consistent with his general strategy. He was willing enough to concede that 'the System', if treated as being no more than an elaborate 'thought-experiment' or model dealing with the inner connections between fundamental logical categories, represented an impressive intellectual achievement. The basic trouble concerned the ontological claims made on its behalf, according to which the concrete sphere of actuality and existence should be viewed as being in some manner expressive of, and dependent upon, the development of what was in essence a self-generating rational process. This move was quite unacceptable and it was ascribable to a 'lunatic postulate' which lay at the heart of the Hegelian doctrine of absolute spirit. Conceptual thinking as ordinarily employed and understood involved abstracting from what was empirically given in reality; moreover, all such abstract thought unavoidably required or presupposed at some point a thinker in the shape of an existing individual. To assert, as Hegel in effect did, that thought was logically prior to existence was to reverse the true order and amounted to reviving, albeit in a confusing and sophistical form, a mode of argument whose fallaciousness had been sufficiently exposed by Kant. The fact that Hegel was able to obscure this, from himself as well as from his readers, was due (it is suggested) to his having supplemented abstract thought and existence by 'a third medium, quite recently discovered'.

The additional medium referred to was something Kierkegaard labelled 'pure thought'. Whereas abstract thought had its source in empirical reality, pure thought apparently managed to dispense with such mundane ties, being an all-encompassing element in terms of which every finite and temporally determined mode of existence, including those relating to ourselves as particular subjects of consciousness and experience, could be comprehended and accounted for: it was indeed on the strength of this 'hypothesis' that the divisions besetting outlooks less developed than Hegel's own were held to be capable finally of resolution, making it possible to affirm the ultimate identity of subject and object and the unity of the human and the divine. But the hypothesis in question was, in a literal sense, fantastic. Concepts that were actually the product of human thinking in its interactions with the world had been falsely endowed with a self-subsistent reality, thought being thereby permitted to 'desert existence' and 'emigrate to a sixth continent where it is wholly sufficient to itself' (CUP 295). Hegel might speak grandly in his *Logic* of giving his system a presuppositionless beginning by starting with the most abstract of all conceptions, namely, that of bare or undifferentiated 'being', and then going on to show how this initiated a dialectical process in which opposed concepts were successively reconciled or synthesized at progressively higher levels; thus at the first stage *being* gave rise to its antithesis, *nothing*, the two being subsequently mediated by the concept of *becoming*. Theoretical transitions between concepts, however, should not be confused with substantial changes occurring in the real world; moreover, Hegel seemingly overlooked the point that all abstract notions, even ones proclaimed to be altogether empty of determinate content, have to be arrived at and entertained by an empirical individual – in the present case, by the speculative philosopher himself who was responsible for the system he constructed and who in other, less exalted contexts was to be found blowing his nose or drawing his salary as a professor. Such considerations, Kierkegaard argues, are in fact fatal to the fiction of a mysterious medium which, 'hovering in mystic suspension between heaven and earth and emancipated from every relation to an existing individual, explains everything in its own terms but fails to explain itself' (CUP 278). The concrete human subject of everyday life, whose existence is necessarily presupposed in all processes of actual reasoning, has been absorbed into the 'shadow-play of pure thought', its place being taken by the chimerical universal subject of metaphysical idealism.

At first sight this might appear to be a strange charge to bring against a thinker who had insisted that world-history was destined to achieve its goal and final consummation within the sphere of specifically human activity and understanding. None the less, it was central to Kierkegaard's vision of Hegel's procedure that in the last analysis it involved inverting the relation of thought to reality, including human beings as part of that reality. For, when all had been said, the latter were pictured as being no more than the manifestations and conscious vehicles of an allegedly 'absolute' reason that transcended them. By thus elevating their rationality to the status of an autonomous and all-embracing spiritual principle, Hegel was vulnerable to a critical approach which he had been ready enough to adopt when discussing other positions. Such criticism could justifiably be turned against his own philosophy.

Conclusions similarly destructive of Hegel's idealist ontology had of course also been reached by Kierkegaard's radical contemporaries in Germany, the Young Hegelians. But they were more receptive to its underlying ambiguity and the morals they drew were very different from his. If the basic priorities of the system were transposed, they believed that it could be construed in a fashion that yielded profound insights concerning man's relation to himself and to the world in which he lived. Thus Hegel's particular conception to the significance and role of religion could be welcomed as correct once it was translated into a suitably purified anthropological idiom; furthermore, and as he himself had implied, many of the general categories and oppositions delineated in his thought were open to an empirical interpretation that illuminated the actual forces governing human development in a social and historical setting. A 'demystifying' form of exegesis along these lines had first been suggested by Feuerbach and it was one whose possibilities other writers, most notably Marx, were quick to recognize and exploit.

Kierkegaard's own response – at least as it emerges in the *Postscript* – stands in sharp contrast to the spirit of such proposals. If Hegel's theory of religion easily lent itself to construals in which man, not God, constituted the true object of the religious consciousness, this could only confirm the point that the so-called 'speculative interpretation' utterly distorted the meaning of Christianity. But in any event he shows no signs of sympathizing with conceptions of the system in which it was viewed as a potential source of valuable truths about the human condition. On the contrary, everything he says here indicates that he felt claims of this sort basically to be misconceived, both in principle and from a practical standpoint. Hegel's philosophy of history could not legitimately be detached from the logical and metaphysical assumptions that inspired and underpinned it. To accept it, therefore, was to be unavoidably – and mistakenly – committed to a deterministic view of the past. The account offered was one that portrayed the historical process as following an ineluctably necessary course; as such, it respected neither the essentially contingent character of historical occurrences nor the freedom of the human agents who participated in them. This, indeed, was something he had already alluded to in the *Fragments*; in the present context, however, he stressed its connection with a further consideration to which he attached the greatest importance. For the Hegelian thesis that history was 'the concretion of the Idea' amounted in effect to the contention that historical periods and societies, regarded as embodying evolving categories of thought or 'principles', should be accorded primacy in any acceptable evaluation of the significance of human affairs; as a result the status of the individual was correspondingly diminished, his role being reduced to that of merely 'representing', or giving particular expression to, the ethos of his age or society.

Kierkegaard believed such a doctrine to be not only perverse in itself but insidious and debilitating in its practical consequences. Psychologically speaking, it accorded with the common tendency to evade personal responsibility and commitment through pretence or self-deception which we have found him attacking elsewhere as symptomatic of a pervasive contemporary *malaise*. People were all too disposed to 'lose themselves in the totality of things, in world-history', sinking their identities in collective notions like those of the spirit of the age or the progress of mankind, and it was part of the appeal of current Hegelianism that it appeared to lend academic respectability to attitudes of this kind. But that was not all. For the doctrine in question could also be seen as giving explicit support to a theory of conduct according to which 'the ethical first finds its concrete embodiment in the world-historical, and becomes in this form a task for the living' (CUP 129): the latter, in other words, were called upon to recognize the 'moral substance' of the historical community to which they belonged and to conform in their actions to this. The ethical was thereby assimilated to the public, the objective. To realize oneself as a moral agent was to acknowledge one's place in an established social order; in following its requirements one would, moreover, achieve what Hegel called one's 'substantive freedom', the self-conscious individual finding himself fulfilled and 'carried out' in the universal.

The conception of ethics referred to here is strongly reminiscent of the one which – at any rate for part of the time – Kierkegaard appeared to have in mind when characterizing the standpoint of morality in such works as *Either/Or* and *Fear and Trembling*. It therefore comes as some surprise to discover him talking throughout the *Postscript* as if such a conception involved a profound misrepresentation of what 'the ethical' is really about. In passage after passage he reiterates the point that ethics is essentially concerned with the individual and his innermost self: 'the sole ethical interest is in one's own reality' (CUP 288). All attempts to externalize or objectify it, whether in the shape of 'world-history' or of socially established rules and norms or of both, are deeply erroneous: the belief that ethical life confirms 'the metaphysical principle . . . that the outward is the inward, the inward the outward, the one wholly commensurable with the other', may have a certain appeal for those caught up in the 'warp and woof' of everyday existence; all the same, it is a 'temptation to be met and conquered' (CUP 123). It is with the 'inner spirit' of the individual person that ethics has pre-eminently to do, and any endeavour to compromise or undermine that paramount insight must be sternly resisted.

What are we to make of this? Although his employment of pseudonyms admittedly tends to complicate matters, it would be hard for even the most sympathetic of Kierkegaard's commentators to contend that his writings are invariably conspicuous for their consistency and precision. In the instance before us, I think that it must be simply accepted that (however confusingly) he construed the category of the ethical in the *Postscript* in a fashion that often seems to be markedly at variance with the portrayal of it which is dominant in those contexts where he was primarily concerned to contrast it with the religious; it is no accident that in the present connection he appears intent upon stressing the continuities between the two spheres than upon pointing up their differences. But the change involved is perhaps less extreme than it might at first glance strike one as being. For one thing, even in his previous discussions of morality he implied that a distinction should be drawn between treating it as a self-sufficient human institution and regarding it instead as deriving its ultimate authority from its being the expression of the divine will. Secondly, it will be remembered that the judge's account of ethics in *Either/Or* at times displayed a notable tension, an ambivalence: there were certainly occasions when it was suggested that depth of conviction, strength of inward or personal commitment, were intrinsic to the moral consciousness in a way that raised doubts as to whether these features could finally be reconciled with conceptions which stressed the social and institutional nature of moral requirements. And it is this strongly individualistic strain that can be said to take precedence in the *Postscript*, governing the treatment accorded to ethics and religion alike. As in the case of the latter, so also – it now emerges – in the case of the former, Hegel stands condemned for having misdescribed and distorted what is at issue:

> Ethics has been crowded out of the System, and as a substitute for it there has been included a something which confuses the historical with the individual, the bewildering and noisy demands of the age with the eternal demand that conscience makes upon the individual. Ethics concentrates upon the individual, and eternally it is the task of every individual to become an entire man.
>
> (CUP 309)

The subjective view

Generally speaking, then, Kierkegaard concluded that Hegel's attempt to substantiate the time-honoured conception of reason as a source of ultimate truth raised insuperable difficulties and was open to fundamental objections. His ambition to comprehend reality under all its various aspects, including those accredited to the moral and religious consciousness, had only been accomplished at the price of a ruinous conflation of categories and the assimilation to one another of matters that should properly be kept apart. Thus existence had been absorbed within thought, the contingent reduced to the necessary, the individual subordinated to the universal. It was, moreover, a corollary of his procedure that he had been led to overlook, or at any rate crucially obscure, the priority of sensory awareness to both the creation of our concepts and the formation of our inferences; traces of an empiricist epistemology, discernible on occasion in the *Fragments*, surface again from time to time in the anti-Hegelian polemics of the *Postscript*. We should be wrong, however, to assume that in the latter work – any more than in the former – Kierkegaard wished to suggest that some alternative approach was available which, while avoiding the sophistry and illusion that infected Hegel's inflated rationalism, might none the less provide Christianity with objective support acceptable to a 'reasonable person' of the kind referred to in Hume's *Enquiry*. The entire notion of providing such backing, whether interpreted in the Hegelian manner or in some other way, was out of place and must be totally rejected. Christianity, we are told, 'protests against every form of objectivity'; subjective acceptance alone is here 'the decisive factor'.

> It is subjectivity that Christianity is concerned with, and it is only in subjectivity that its truth exists, if it exists at all; objectively, Christianity has absolutely no existence.
>
> (CUP 116)

With the idea of subjectivity, and the conception of truth he associated with it, we can in fact be said to have reached the pivot on which Kierkegaard's account of religious belief in the *Postscript* finally turns. Faith, he insists, 'inheres in subjectivity' and constitutes its 'highest passion'; it is only by 'becoming subjective' that the import of Christianity can be grasped and appropriated in a way that makes it a reality for the believer. Yet his treatment of the concept is a complex and elusive one, and it has not unnaturally occasioned a great deal of controversy. What has he in mind and how does it bear upon some of the points previously raised? These are not easy questions to answer, a principal reason being that in his approach to the topic he was influenced by a number of distinguishable considerations.

One such consideration, which can be picked out as playing a central role, focused upon the contrast between the standpoint of the agent and the standpoint of the spectator. The French philosopher, Emmanuel Mounier (1905–50), once characterized existentialism as 'a reaction of the philosophy of man against the excesses of the philosophy of ideas and the philosophy of things'. This remark is certainly apposite so far as Kierkegaard is concerned. As we saw in chapter 3, he maintained that it was an illusion to suppose that all aspects of human life and experience could be accommodated within the kind of perspective afforded by detached or observational modes of thought. In a fashion that in some respects invites comparison with the Kantian distinction between the theoretical and practical points of view, he sought to underline the profound gulf that separates two stances which it is possible to adopt in our dealings with reality – the disengaged stance of contemplation and objective enquiry and the engaged or participatory stance of agency and practical volition. There could be no objection to adopting the former within the boundaries set by particular disciplines or branches of study, such as mathematics, history, or the physical sciences. Misconceptions, however, arose when the spectatorial or external attitude was allowed to spread beyond its proper limits, engulfing everything within its scope and leading the individual to lose sight of his distinctive character as a particular centre of action and choice. This happened whether, as in the case of speculative idealism, he was pictured as being a mere vehicle of absolute spirit or whether, as with certain scientifically inspired forms of materialism, he was conceived as no more than a component of a causally regulated universe, ultimately governed by laws and forces beyond his control; a view of the latter sort might perhaps be ascribed to Spinoza but it was more obviously attributable to some representatives of the French Enlightenment. Yet, whatever their provenance, all such positions falsified or fatally obscured a perspective that was indispensable to us when considered in our capacity as active self-conscious subjects, each with a particular life to lead and particular decisions to take. To suppose that we could assume a transcendent standpoint of the kind envisaged was to lack a true appreciation of what it meant to be a human being confronting problems that called for personal choice rather than ones answerable to impersonal investigation. As Kierkegaard put it in a well-known journal entry of 1843, in this sense we could find no Archimedean 'resting-place':

> It is perfectly true, as philosophers say, that life must be understood backwards. But they forget the other proposition, that it must be lived forwards.

> (J 127)

That there are cardinal differences between the ways in which we think when we are regarding things 'from the outside' as uninvolved spectators or enquirers and the outlook we adopt 'from within' as agents committed to form and seek to realize specific intentions seems hard to dispute. And in his stress on subjectivity Kierkegaard may partly be interpreted as wishing to reinstate and accentuate the significance of the perspective of practical engagement in the face of those who either ignored it or sought to explain it away; we cannot view everything, including ourselves and our actions, under some purely observational or explanatory aspect. He did not wish to deny that people often proceeded as if this were not so, treating themselves as conforming to objective categories or descriptions and consequently as being somehow bound to behave in determinate ways: thus they might, as in certain expressions of the aesthetic consciousness, see themselves as endowed with an unalterable character; again, they might identify themselves with a particular role or even (on at any rate some interpretations of the ethical) conceive of themselves as being inescapably obliged to follow socially recognized rules and duties. All such conceptions, however, involved types of self-deception which it

13. Jean-Paul Sartre (1905–1980).

was necessary to uncover and expose, and in drawing attention to them Kierkegaard may justly be credited with having anticipated the analyses of inauthenticity and *mauvaise foi* which have figured so prominently in later existentialist literature. It was not for nothing that Sartre, in particular, maintained that the 'subjectivity of the individual' constituted his point of departure, insisting on the need to recognize what it entailed and to understand that responsibility for what we were or did could not be sloughed off on to some supposedly objective determinant.

This theme is clearly discernible in Kierkegaard's work and variations on it recur throughout the *Postscript*. Even so, in his case there was more at stake. It is one thing to assert that we cannot live merely as observers and that the claims of the subjective perspective as it features in agency must be lucidly confronted in any adequate portrayal of our situation in the world. It is another to write as if in the last analysis that perspective should be accorded precedence. And it is another thing again to argue that it is only by reference to such a viewpoint that the significance of ethics and religion alike can be rightly apprehended. Both of these further contentions help to define his own distinctive position; both, too, are associated with an attempt to differentiate between the two dimensions of experience in a way that seems to be more extreme in some of its implications than the one so far considered.

Much that is said on the last score has puzzled commentators, Kierkegaard speaking at times as if the character of objective reflection, with its use of general terms and ideas, inevitably precluded it from achieving a grasp of the essential particularity of existence, and as if it was only through the inner consciousness of agency that we became truly apprised of the latter. None the less, although his mode of expressing himself often appears exaggerated or misleading, it is not too difficult to appreciate the underlying preoccupations that prompted him. In the final resort it was with ourselves, distinguished from the rest of nature as responsible and self-determining participants in the 'existential process' that he was concerned. Moreover, it was central to his vision of the human condition that we should lead our lives in a way that required us to be continuously attentive to our ultimate worth and destiny as individual persons; by comparison, all other considerations – including those relating to cognitive or theoretical enquiry – fell away and could be seen finally to be irrelevant or distracting. His stress on 'inwardness', which was integral to what he meant by subjectivity, mirrored this emphasis. Inwardness was not to be equated with a habit of introspective reflection on our own mental states; that would make it a mode of detached contemplation, not of active involvement, and would amount to assimilating it to the observational outlook Kierkegaard associated with objectivity. Rather, it manifests itself in self-commitment and the spirit in which such commitment is undertaken: a person exhibits inwardness through the resolutions he forms, the sincerity with which he identifies with them, and the degree to which they govern his approach to the situations that confront him. So understood, it is intimately connected with the conception of the ethical dominant in the *Postscript*, in which singleness of mind and purpose is contrasted with social conformism and where the obligation to abide by one's innermost convictions as an individual is held to override any calculations of contingent upshot or historical outcome. But that is not all. For it also turns out to be essential to the account which is given there of religious, and pre-eminently of Christian, faith. Faith, too, presupposes inwardness as a fundamental condition. In the light of the foregoing this suggests that action rather than cognitive thought is the appropriate category to which it should be assigned. And much that Kierkegaard says about it appears to invite such an interpretation. He goes out of his way to reiterate the claim that Christianity is not a matter of 'objective knowledge', as if belief in it amounted to the kind of disinterested assent we might accord to a mathematical demonstration or scientific hypothesis. On the contrary, it requires a passionate and resolute engagement of the whole personality, intensity of involvement being the crucial thing. Here, as before, the stress seems to be upon personal dedication, the manner and frame of mind in which a certain course is entered upon and sustained.

The view that religious faith is not merely a matter of assenting to particular propositions but also demands commitment to a particular mode of living is hardly likely to provoke dispute. Kierkegaard was not alone in insisting that it should make a profound difference to the overall tone and character of a person's life, even if he felt justified in accusing representatives of contemporary 'Christendom' of conspicuously failing to measure up to this requirement. More controversial, on the other hand, would be the contention that acting in the light of certain deeply held ideals and engaging in certain practices is *all* that it need legitimately be held to comprise, its basic tenets being more properly taken to be expressive of a moral vision or to embody spiritual values than as constituting assertions that purport to be true in some literal or specifically factual sense. Yet such a position, anticipations of which can indeed already be found in the writings of some Enlightenment theorists, is not without its modern adherents. While frequently differing in their positive construals, certain recent Christian thinkers have implied that propositions concerning, for example, the nature of God or of personal immortality should not be treated as involving determinate truth-claims about a transcendent or supernatural reality; instead, they are best understood in a 'non-realist' and practically orientated way, and as playing a regulative rather than a descriptive or predictive role in religious contexts. It follows that efforts to substantiate them on the assumption that they represent straightforwardly factual assertions will be misconceived. Critics like Hume and Kant may have successfully discredited attempts of the latter sort. Their objections, however, need no longer be considered to touch the actual concerns of faith, although in raising them they may have indirectly helped to draw attention to the true bearing of those concerns.

Kierkegaard's name is sometimes invoked by philosophers sympathetic to the above line of thought. His deployment of voluntaristic and emotional concepts to portray the standpoint of religious belief seems at first sight wholly consonant with positions that interpret it as being a matter of practical concern and conative attitude rather than of cognitive acceptance. Moreover, what he says about the essential irrelevance of demands for objective proof or evidential assurance in this connection is apparently echoed by modern writers who condemn such demands as betraying a misunderstanding of the real significance of religious statements. But surface similarities can conceal deeper differences. However strongly he may have stressed the active dimension of faith and however contemptuously he dismissed endeavours to provide it with a rational foundation, it remains hard to see how he could have avoided regarding approaches of the type referred to as exemplifying yet another attempt to escape the challenge he thought Christianity presented. For by attenuating what it ostensibly proclaimed in the proposed fashion, would they not in effect be robbing it of the very feature he wished above all to stress?

In the *Postscript* Kierkegaard never in fact departs from the thesis, central to the argument of the *Fragments*, that Christianity is inherently paradoxical, resistant to human reason. It is true that in the later work he is at pains to distinguish between different levels or stages of the religious consciousness; it is also true that the distinctions drawn are not always sharply or systematically observed, with the consequence that the reader may on occasions feel unsure as to how exactly the relation between faith and reason is meant to be interpreted. Thus he writes at times as if belief in the existence of God and the promise of an eternal happiness involves embracing an 'objective uncertainty' simply in the sense of there being here a necessary absence of rational proof or even of probability. Where there is objective certainty or security, he says, there can be no question of venture and where there is no possibility of venture there can be no faith; faith, indeed, is stated to be 'precisely the contradiction between the infinite passion of the individual's inwardness and the objective uncertainty' – it is a question of being 'out upon the deep, over seventy thousand fathoms of water' (CUP 182). He indicates, none the less, that faith for a Christian requires considerably more than this. For it demands of the individual that he 'risk his thought', venturing to believe *against* the understanding. Christianity, we are told,

> has proclaimed itself as the *Paradox*, and it has required of the individual the inwardness of faith in relation to that which stamps itself as an offence to the Jews and a folly to the Greeks – and an absurdity to the understanding.
>
> (CUP 191)

Nor are we left in doubt that it is once again the reality of the incarnation that Kierkegaard principally has in mind. As he puts it elsewhere, that 'that which in accordance with its nature is eternal comes into existence in time, is born, grows up, and dies – this is a breach with all thinking' (CUP 513).

Passages like these make it amply clear that there is no retraction of the position which had been enunciated earlier. The repudiation by faith of the claims of rationality is reaffirmed with – if anything – additional force; Christianity specifically involves relinquishing the 'natural' discriminations of the finite understanding and taking a 'qualitative leap' into the realm of the intellectually opaque or repellent (CUP 159, 343). What, on the other hand, is markedly less in evidence is the notion, previously stressed in the *Fragments*, that it also requires as an enabling condition some kind of inner transformation through the miraculous power of divine grace. Instead, the focus of attention in the *Postscript* – where the main concern is said to be with what it means to *become* a Christian – tends to centre almost exclusively upon the stance adopted by the human subject. And here it seems that holding certain things to be actually the case in the face of rational difficulties and objections is treated as being as much a matter of personal involvement or dedication as holding fast to a practical commitment or policy, the situation of the believer in such circumstances being portrayed in a fashion often highly evocative of that of an individual confronting contrary inclinations at the level of intentional action. This impression may, moreover, be strengthened if we take into account Kierkegaard's distinctive, albeit somewhat cryptically worded, contention that action in the strict sense of the term should be differentiated from the external or publicly observable behaviour it initiates; properly understood, it is confined to the 'internal' decision through which a person identifies himself existentially with what he previously entertained only notionally (CUP 302A). All in all, then, it might appear that, far from seeking to play down or eliminate the significance of the transcendent or supernatural content of faith, Kierkegaard sought rather to emphasize the affinities between its propositional and practical aspects while at the same time making unmistakably plain the gulf that divided the subjective orientation of the religious consciousness from the detached perspective characteristic of objective thought and enquiry. In Christian belief, which demands acceptance of what is from a rational standpoint uncertain or even absurd, inwardness is 'intensified to the utmost degree'; as such, it can be said to constitute 'the highest passion in the sphere of human subjectivity' (CUP 118). What is more, it can also be said to constitute the truth. 'Subjectivity', Kierkegaard subsequently and insistently goes on to reiterate, 'is the truth.'

The truth of subjectivity

It is hardly to be wondered at if the famous dictum just quoted has induced a sense of vertigo amongst some readers of the *Postscript*. Ordinarily we are disposed to associate questions of truth or falsity with questions about how things as a matter of fact stand, independently of what anyone – however passionately – may feel about them. Does Kierkegaard seriously wish to oppose this common conception, replacing it by an altogether different one? If so, what alternative does he envisage? If not, what exactly does the proclaimed identity of truth with subjectivity amount to?

In a passage whose importance is emphasized in the text, he refers to two distinct ways in which the issue of truth may arise.

> When the question of truth is raised in an objective manner, reflection is directed objectively to the truth, as an object to which the knower is related ... If only the object to which he is related is the truth, the subject is accounted to be in the truth. When the question of truth is raised subjectively, reflection is directed subjectively to the nature of the individual's relationship; if only the mode of this relationship is in the truth, the individual is in the truth even if he should happen to be thus related to what is not true.
>
> (CUP 178)

In elaboration of what he means, Kierkegaard stresses the need to differentiate between two modes of assessing a belief; these concern its 'what' and its 'how'. 'The objective accent falls on *what* is said, the subjective accent on *how* it is said'; and so far at least as religious belief is concerned it seems that he regards the latter mode as being the fundamental one. Thus, in a further well-known passage, he compares the situation of one man who, though having a 'true conception' of God, prays to him in a 'false spirit' with that of another who, though he belongs to an idolatrous community, prays to his idol with 'the entire passion of the infinite'. According to Kierkegaard, it is at the side of the second man, not the first, that 'most truth' is to be found – 'the one prays in truth to God, though he worships an idol; the other prays falsely to the true God, and hence worships in fact an idol' (CUP 180).

Despite certain oddities of formulation, Kierkegaard's main point here seems to centre upon an ambiguity in the notion of truly believing something. In one sense it can be taken to mean that what is believed corresponds to what is actually the case, while in the other it refers to the fashion in which the belief is subscribed to, that is, to its being genuinely or deeply held; being 'subjectively' in the truth is essentially a matter of believing in the second of these senses. But on this interpretation his equation of truth with subjectivity might appear to come to little more than a re-endorsement of the value of the personal involvement and passionate commitment he associated with inwardness. So understood, it would seemingly permit any believer to be counted as in the truth provided only that he was appropriately wedded to his belief and irrespective of what that belief happened to be. And if that is the most that the attribution of truth to Christian faith is intended to convey, it may be felt to be somewhat limited in the assurance it offers. For truth in this sense could presumably be ascribed with as much justification to the convictions of an atheist as to those of a theist if the former's attachment to his atheism was sufficiently profound and unqualified. Given Kierkegaard's own declared subscription to the tenets of Christianity, which (as we have just seen) allowed him confidently to distinguish between the 'true God' and an idol, it may seem hard to suppose that he had nothing more positive in mind.

There are, indeed, intimations of a different interpretation. For one thing, Kierkegaard was unfailingly insistent upon the unique character of the subjective acceptance of Christianity; inwardness achieves maximal intensity in the case of an individual who genuinely commits himself to its paradoxical claims. For another, he appears – on occasions at least – to imply that the very degree of passion or intensity involved may serve as a guarantee that these claims are in fact objectively true. Thus he says in a journal entry of December 1849, with apparent reference to the *Postscript*, that if the 'how' of faith is given, its 'what' is also given, adding that here 'we have inwardness at its maximum proving to be objectivity' (J 355). And in the *Postscript* itself, after dismissing 'systematic' attempts to prove personal immortality, he indicates that we should turn to subjectivity instead – immortality is stated to be the 'most passionate interest' of subjectivity, and 'precisely in the interest lies the proof' (CUP 155). Such remarks might understandably be taken to mean that the strength of commitment and aspiration intrinsic to belief in Christianity is by itself sufficient to ensure the validity of its factual content; through following the 'way of subjectivity' we can gain a veridical insight that is necessarily unattainable by pursuing the endless 'road of approximation' to which the impersonal procedures of objective enquiry confine us.

The trouble with the above line of thought is that it remains quite unclear how subjective conviction or passionate aspiration alone can ever certify the reality of what is believed in or aspired to. This has caused one critic to complain that the view alluded to involves a transparent *non sequitur* and to accuse Kierkegaard of misleadingly amalgamating it with the weaker and factually noncommittal position mentioned previously, where the 'truth' ascribed to faith consisted merely in the depth of inwardness it entailed; in consequence, it may be tempting to imagine that he somehow managed to underwrite Christian belief in a fashion that was impervious to the objections levelled against traditional forms of validation or support. As a diagnosis of fallacies attributable to some of Kierkegaard's latter-day followers, the criticism has considerable force. Nor can it be denied that he himself is apt to give the impression of being precariously poised between disparate positions, leaving it uncertain which of them he actually holds. In the end, however, one may wonder how far the various difficulties and obscurities surrounding what he writes on this score really impinge upon his fundamental aims. Notwithstanding intermittent suggestions to the contrary, it is arguable that here, as elsewhere, his purpose was essentially expository, being directed to articulating the conceptual and phenomenological implications of faith rather than to providing it with any kind of epistemic justification. On such an account, his central concern remained one of assigning religious belief to the sphere to which in his opinion it properly belonged, the sphere, namely, of personal choice and involvement as opposed to that of detached reflection and appraisal; it is possible, indeed, to understand his assertion (cited earlier) that the truth of Christianity exists 'only in subjectivity' as no more than a way of expressing this point. As he constantly reminds us, it is of the essence of faith as he conceives it that it constitutes a personal venture or risk, a wholehearted and passionate determination to accept something in the full consciousness that it lies beyond the reach of all intellectual demonstration and any sort of objective warrant. At the same time, to adopt such a course must surely be to presuppose that there is a genuine issue regarding the reality of what is thus accepted. But in so committing oneself, one can hardly be taken to be thereby resolving that issue; where otherwise would be the crucial element of risk it is acknowledged to involve?

If we follow this interpretation, however, we inevitably encounter other questions. The notion – recurrent in Kierkegaard's writings – that belief is subject to the will is notoriously a problematic one in philosophy, and it is suggestive of further ambiguities. We can certainly decide to act *as if* we believed a particular proposition to be true, leaving the matter of its actual truth-value – provisionally at least – undetermined; that is clear enough and can frequently be allowed to occur. It is also conceivable (as Pascal noted) that perseverance in such action may have the consequence that we eventually come to believe the proposition in fact and not merely hypothetically. What is less obvious is that we can, consciously and directly, set ourselves to believe something *tout court*, irrespective of any grounds we might have for supposing it to be true and even perhaps in the face of what we see to be overwhelming evidence to the contrary. These difficulties are, moreover, compounded if what we are asked to believe is stated to be inherently paradoxical – not only lacking in objective foundation, but intrinsically unacceptable or 'offensive' from a rational standpoint. In what sense can I undertake to believe something which I recognize to be literally unthinkable, a contradiction 'in opposition to all human reason'? Yet it is to the feasibility of doing just that that Kierkegaard seems to be committed when he roundly rejects the idea that Christian belief has anything to do with probability, in whatever degree, and declares instead that the object of faith is 'the absurd' (CUP 189).

To meet the implied objection it may be suggested that he could have invoked the notion of an enabling condition afforded by grace which figured so prominently in the *Fragments*; an inner transformation of the kind postulated would make it possible for an individual to accept what from the circumscribed vantage-point of human rationality appears incredible. If, however, Kierkegaard's references to 'the absurd' are supposed to identify something held to be literally inconsistent or self-contradictory, it is unclear that such a proposal addresses what is really at issue in the present context. For that concerns the very intelligibility of the claim that one can believe what one at the same time recognizes to be necessarily or demonstrably false. Consequently some commentators have inferred that he cannot have actually intended to propound so idiosyncratic a thesis, opting instead for less extreme versions of his position. It has been maintained, for instance, that his conception of absurdity need not after all be construed as implying more than the absence of rational support; to say that, in response to the promise of eternal salvation held out by Christianity, we must make an all-out commitment to a mystery that transcends the categories of reason is not to say that we are required to believe what we clearly perceive to be contrary to it. Alternatively, it has been argued that for Kierkegaard the paradox of the incarnation essentially consisted in its being an offence to our sentiments rather than to our understanding: God is felt to have appeared in a shockingly inappropriate form and to have suffered humiliations and indignities unworthy of his divine nature. There are certainly passages in various of Kierkegaard's works, and particularly in *Training in Christianity*, which are consonant with the latter approach. Even so much that he wrote in the *Postscript* indicates that this was by no means all that he had in mind. He may have portrayed the incarnation as emotionally or morally outrageous in the sense of dumbfounding standard expectations or upsetting commonly accepted valuations; but the conclusion that he wanted to stress its offensiveness to the intellect as well seems irresistible in the light of his frequent asseverations to that effect. It was surely not for nothing that, when speaking of the 'martyrdom' of faith, he referred to it as a 'crucifixion of the understanding'.

Chapter 6
Freedom and the self

Whatever room there may be for disagreement as to the precise sense or senses in which Kierkegaard held Christianity to be paradoxical, one thing at least seems beyond dispute: he never diverged from the claim that its ultimate significance could only be grasped through personal appropriation and inner commitment. Thus, in seeking to disentangle the notion of faith from the assorted misconceptions that in his view had served to obscure its essential character, he may be said to have returned once more to a category which, in a variety of connections, we have found to constitute the touchstone of his thinking – the category of the particular human subject, the 'existing individual'. He went out of his way to praise Socrates for being (albeit in a pagan context) the first to have introduced that crucial conception 'with decisive dialectical force'; and he himself took pride in having set out to reaffirm and highlight its importance in a contemporary climate where he felt that people in general were either devoid of all insight into what it meant or else at pains to shut their eyes to its actual implications. Yet questions certainly remain as to how he supposed that this category should be understood in a specifically Christian perspective. Who is the 'I', lonely and responsible, that stands at the centre of the Kierkegaardian universe? What are its needs and how can they be satisfied? A brief consideration of themes developed in two of his writings – *The Concept of Anxiety* and *The Sickness unto Death* – may help to illustrate some of the issues raised.

Although the above books are often referred to as Kierkegaard's 'psychological works', a modern reader who approaches them in the expectation that they will conform to more familiar enquiries of this nature is liable to be disconcerted. Not only do they contain frequent allusions to such ideas as innocence, sin, and redemption; they are also written in a philosophically orientated style that is often dense and difficult to penetrate. Abstractions abound and Kierkegaard does not always trouble to explain the abstruse terminology he has chosen to employ. In consequence, there are passages which produce a bafflement comparable to that induced by the more opaque sections of Hegel's *Phenomenology of Mind*. Yet this, one may surmise, is not wholly accidental. Despite his well-advertised hostility to the German thinker's conclusions, Kierkegaard was not averse to drawing upon concepts and distinctions which the latter had favoured, even if it meant putting them to very different purposes. Moreover, Hegel had deployed some of these to characterize a situation with which he himself was centrally concerned, and I follow other commentators in thinking that his own treatment of it should initially be considered against the Hegelian background.

The situation in question was one that Hegel associated with religion and which he attributed to 'the unhappy consciousness'. As we saw in chapter 2, this expression was introduced to designate a certain stage in the course of man's historical development. At such a stage he was aware of himself as a divided being, 'dual-natured' and 'inwardly disrupted'. On the one hand, he was conscious of himself as a finite particular, located in the world of experience and subject to the vicissitudes of temporal change; on the other, he was haunted by the thought of possessing an 'unchangeable' or ideal essence that subsisted independently of the contingencies which beset his empirical reality. These two aspects of his nature he was unable to bring together with the result that he identified himself with the first, apprehending the second under the form of a transcendent 'other' or 'alien Being' to which he stood opposed and with which he sought to be reconciled.

Such a conception of his condition was, however, a deceptive one; its true import would become apparent when the human mind ultimately overcame its self-estrangement in immature modes of life and consciousness and when it was in a position to recognize both itself and the world it inhabited as manifestations of an infinite or absolute rational essence whose potentialities could only be realized in and through the medium of the finite.

There is no need to rehearse Kierkegaard's objections to the idealist metaphysic in terms of which this diagnosis of the sources and underlying content of religious ideas was propounded, his own approach being presented within a framework that presupposed rather than purported to supersede the dualistic outlook of traditional theism. At the same time, though, and not perhaps surprisingly, polarities of the kind that had informed Hegel's discussion of the particular standpoint of the unhappy consciousness tended to dominate the account he himself gave of the status and aspirations of the individual in a religious context. Not only was the antithesis between the finite and the eternal, the human and the divine, treated by him as ontologically fundamental; in the final analysis it also governed the picture he drew of human nature and its basic orientation.

Following what we found to be the general tenor of the *Postscript*, with its emphasis upon the lived perspective of agency and choice, Kierkegaard's psychological writings portray the structure of the human personality in dynamic and volitional terms. From one point of view a human being may be described as 'a synthesis of the psychical and the physical', an intimate conjunction of mental and bodily characteristics; so conceived, he can be said to belong together with the rest of the world as a type of entity distinguished by the possession of certain determinate attributes. But to regard an individual solely in that light is to lose sight of the fact that he is able to transcend his natural traits and circumstances and that he must also be understood as 'spirit' – a crucial dimension which Kierkegaard connects with the notion of acquiring a 'self' and which underlies his notoriously cryptic definition of the latter concept as 'a relation that relates itself to its own self' (SD 13). Although much time and labour has since been spent in trying to decide what exactly he meant by that curious form of words, I shall confine myself here simply to giving what I take to be part of the upshot of the tortuous discussion in which it is embedded. To be a person is to exist in the mode, not of being, but of becoming, and what a person becomes is his own responsibility, the product of his will, even if (as is frequently the case) this is something he does not want to confront and seeks to conceal from himself. Moreover, every individual can be held to be aware – whether actually or potentially – of a tension between his current conception of his condition and the presence of alternatives that are in some sense available to him; as it is put at one point, there is not a living being who 'does not secretly harbour an unrest, an inner strife, a disharmony, . . . an anxiety about some possibility in existence or an anxiety about himself' (SD 22). Such disturbing intimations and attitudes, however, should not be thought of as restricted to particular phases of history and as destined to disappear when the human mind eventually finds itself (in Hegel's reassuring phrase) 'at home' in the world. On the contrary, Kierkegaard considers them to be revelatory of our intrinsic character as persons and to feature, in one form or another, in the life-story of every individual. In this way they are constant and pervasive, endemic to the human condition. But, if so, what according to him is the true significance of the kind of unease or disquiet to which he refers?

Kierkegaard's conception of anxiety or dread (*Angst*) is famous, partly through its undeniable influence upon 20th-century philosophers like Sartre and Heidegger, and partly too because it has been felt to throw into striking relief certain apparently 'objectless' states of mind that are recognizable at the level of ordinary experience. The account he gives of it is, moreover, a complex and far-reaching one, covering a wide range of phenomena that includes both childhood preoccupations with the mysterious or uncanny and later premonitions connected with the

14. The 'dizziness of freedom'; a bungee jumper attracted and repelled by the 'possibility of being able'.

awakening of the sexual impulse. The variety of aspects under which the notion is discussed may, indeed, help to explain the impression his analysis has made on thinkers of very different ideological persuasions, many of whom have been far from sharing the particular standpoint from which it was undertaken.

One of these aspects, implicit in the passage quoted above, has to do with the awareness of freedom. Kierkegaard makes it clear, early in his book on the subject, that anxiety in the sense that interests him should not be confused with emotions like fear, which have a definite object and are typically directed to things or occurrences in the outside world; by contrast, it is said to be related to 'something that is nothing' and to represent 'freedom's actuality as the possibility of possibility' (CA 42–3). In an explicit reference to Kierkegaard's distinction, Sartre maintained that anxiety so construed is essentially 'anxiety (*angoisse*) before myself': I am not, as in the case of fear, concerned with what will happen to me as the passive victim of circumstances; rather, the condition in question derives from my consciousness of myself as an active subject who can envisage and respond to possibilities and where there is nothing that objectively compels me to opt for one response as opposed to another – here I am the sole arbiter and what I do is entirely up to me. Sartre invokes the example of vertigo, where a person is said to be not so much afraid of falling over a precipice as affected by the thought that he can if he chooses 'throw himself over'; and this is reminiscent – no doubt designedly – of an image that Kierkegaard himself employs when he compares anxiety with the feeling aroused by looking down into a yawning abyss. Thus it is characterized by him in one place as the 'dizziness of freedom', something that occurs when 'freedom looks down into its own possibility, laying hold of finiteness to support itself' (CA 61). Again, Kierkegaard refers to it elsewhere as 'a *sympathetic antipathy* and an *antipathetic sympathy*'; the subject is pictured as standing ambivalently poised, at once attracted and repelled by the disturbing 'possibility of *being able*' (CA 42ff.).

The air of urgency and tension that infects such descriptions anticipates the heightened tone of a good deal of later existentialist writing on this theme, a tone which has often provoked the criticism that it reflects a recurrent tendency to inflate or over-dramatize the significance of large tracts of everyday thought and behaviour. But whatever the conceivable force of such criticism in other connections, Kierkegaard would certainly have rejected its relevance to his own position. Sartre's portrayal of anxiety in the face of freedom may succeed in capturing part of what he had in mind; nevertheless, he himself was primarily concerned with what he held to be its religious import. And so approached, it involved considerations which were of a different order from those adduced by his more secularly minded successors and which he believed to be of the greatest moment for our development and eventual fate as human beings.

Anxiety in fact first appears in his account in the context of a discussion of original sin. In the biblical story of the fall Adam is presented as being ignorant initially of the difference between good and evil and of all that it entails; even so, the prohibition that he should not eat the fruit of the tree of knowledge 'awakens in him the possibility of freedom'. Kierkegaard treats the story as illustrating in mythic form the manner in which the transition from a state of 'unselfconscious immediacy' to one of self-awareness and self-determination arises in the experience of every individual. Innocence is a state in which 'the spirit in man is dreaming': although he has as yet no knowledge of what he might spiritually do or become, he is none the less troubled by an indeterminate presentiment of his potentialities as a free being with the capacity to shape himself and his future – 'this is the profound secret of innocence, that it is at the same time anxiety' (CA 41). But what are the potentialities in question and how does the individual become apprised of their character? As Kierkegaard presents the situation, it appears that he can initially only do so through the experience of sin. Thus the primordial anxiety of which he speaks is said to be the precondition or 'presupposition' of sin, without thereby constituting its necessitating cause; the latter is not susceptible to any kind of deterministic or scientific explanation, everyone becoming guilty 'only through himself'. It would be incorrect, on the other hand, to suppose that the possibility of sin is all that such anxiety portends. For it also obscurely prefigures a recognition of the fact that the resources of a person's finite disposition are capable of being directed along quite different paths and that the realization of his true identity as an individual self lies in his relating, not to temporal or earthly preoccupations which deflect him from his proper goal, but to the eternal, the divine. Rightly understood, human existence takes the form of a 'constant striving', seeking a fulfilment that lies beyond the temporal sphere and which is only attainable by our freely committing ourselves to a power that transcends objective knowledge and rational comprehension; in so 'willing to be itself, the self rests transparently in the power that established it' (SD 49, 131). But this, Kierkegaard asserts, is 'the formula for faith'. Hence it is possible for anxiety to issue in a 'qualitative leap' that takes us, not into sin and alienation from God, but into its antithesis: faith, not virtue, is the 'opposite of sin' (SD 82). In other words, we are returned once more to what Kierkegaard here calls 'Christianity's crucial criterion' – the acceptance of an objective uncertainty that is inaccessible to reason but through which, with divine help, salvation is alone to be found.

The above represents the barest skeleton of an intricate discussion that is chiefly distinguished by its emphasis upon the diversity of ways in which people may fail to realize themselves in the required sense. A Hegelian critic would doubtless have questioned the validity of the notion of self-realization involved, given the limitations it apparently imposes upon a person's fulfilment of needs and interests that are his as a member of the world; moreover, its positive content – perhaps inevitably in the context – remains elusive and finally mysterious. Nevertheless, Kierkegaard is often praised for his insight into various types of spiritual disequilibrium and malaise, and both of the so-called psychological works are in fact studded with concrete examples that frequently display a sharp percipience. This is especially evident when he

Sören Kierkegaard in later years

Woodcut by H. P. Hansen

15. Portrait of Kierkegaard wearing a hat.

is dealing with the tranquillizing or diversionary expedients by which people attempt to hide from themselves the nature of the despair that haunts them. In his treatment of such cases, which recalls diagnoses of the sort offered earlier in books like *Either/Or*, he exploits to the full his exceptional talent for identifying the illusions or defences that obstruct self-knowledge and self-understanding; he is also at pains to distinguish these from instances where, through pride or defiance, a person may consciously reject the possibilities of change and salvation open to him – here 'there is no obscurity that could serve as a mitigating excuse' (SD 42). As so often, the compelling quality and force of many of the observations made seem to bear the imprint of conflicts and crises encountered in his own private experience and recorded in his journals. All the same, difficulties arise in assessing everything he says on this score. To some extent they stem from the tendency, characteristic of much of his work, to handle key concepts with a flexibility that leaves the boundaries of their application shifting or unclear. Thus the notion of despair, central to *The Sickness unto Death*, appears on occasions to be employed in a relatively restricted manner continuous with its ordinary usage; more typically, though, it seems to cover – albeit with significant variations – almost any condition that excludes the presence of faith. No doubt that is in turn connected with the fact that his psychology was elaborated inside a framework whose parameters were ultimately set by the religious point of view from which he was writing. It is assumed, rather than argued, that human nature is so structured that an individual can only free himself from despair and fulfil his fundamental aspirations as a person by embracing the Christian message. This means, however, that in interpreting Kierkegaard's claims the line between what counts as genuinely empirical analysis and what looks more like *a priori* stipulation is not always easy to draw.

Chapter 7
Conclusion

In much of this book I have been concerned to stress the challenge Kierkegaard's thought offered to various intellectual tendencies of his age, particularly those that aimed to reduce the doctrinal content of Christianity to terms that rendered it transparent to human reason. But it would, of course, be wrong to suggest that such a challenge constituted the whole of his religious purpose. As we saw earlier, he was at least equally intent upon resisting what he believed to be a widespread disposition, encouraged by representatives of the Danish Church, to emasculate the Christian message by refusing to confront its import at the level of practical life and motivation. It was not sufficient to participate in established rituals, nor again was it enough admiringly to repeat Christ's words; it was necessary to abide by that he said, to follow him. In his explicitly Christian writings and discourses, which were for the most part published under his own name and which accompanied the more theoretical pseudonymous ones, Kierkegaard set out to accentuate the severity of Christianity's call upon the individual. The covert worldliness and hypocrisy that characterized 'Christendom' must be ruthlessly exposed; and works like *Purity of Heart* and *Training in Christianity* were expressly designed to make manifest what it really meant to 'die to the world' and to set aside all 'relative ends' in an undivided dedication to God's will. Here no compromise was admissible, and every effort to dilute or water down the nature of the temporal sacrifices demanded amounted to evasion and 'double-mindedness'. It is true that his own interpretation of the Christian ideal has led some critics to accuse him of playing down its compassionate and communal aspects and of laying a too exclusive emphasis on personal salvation; although such objections are partly belied by books like *Works of Love*, where love of one's fellow humans is stated to be 'the only blessed consolation' and something without which one is not 'really living', it remains undeniable that the prevailing tone is often narrowly austere and even harsh. At the same time, however, it is worth remembering that much of what he wrote in this connection was, as one commentator, Louis Mackey, has put it, 'informed by the rhetoric of awakening'; he wanted 'to stun men into a salutary awareness of the absolute claim of Christianity and to remind them of their own defection from this claim'. And if the minatory and increasingly sombre note struck by some of his 'reminders', with their insistence upon the ubiquity of guilt and the necessity of suffering, has disconcerted a number of his readers, this would certainly not have surprised him. He can hardly be said to have underestimated the capacity of Christianity – at least as he understood it – to occasion offence. So understood, moreover, it was always open to the individual to reject it if he chose.

For Kierkegaard never explicitly departed from the contention that commitment to a Christian way of life, like commitment to other modes of existence, was in the last analysis a matter of individual decision, something that each person must freely undertake for himself without the possibility of objective justification. Admittedly, his position on this point suffers on occasions from apparent ambiguity. In his theoretical work it is not invariably clear whether he conceives himself to be simply exhibiting what is involved in a given approach or outlook, underlining its implications for those who adopt it, or whether he at times takes himself to be expressing privileged insights which transcend particular standpoints and can legitimately lay claim to some kind of independent validity: such tensions have been noticed in the course of discussing his views about truth and they are also discernible elsewhere. Nevertheless, there can be little question that the notion of radical or ultimate choice remained central to his picture of the human situation, and it is one that has proved influential in the spheres both of ethical theory and of religious thought. At the secular level it has played a contributory role in engendering the conviction, common to a wide range of existentialist writers, that moral judgement can never finally be more than an exercise of personal decision; in their view at least, it is an illusion to imagine that there is a discoverable realm of objective values subsisting independently of ourselves, while to appeal instead for support to institutionalized or socially accepted codes of conduct is to be in danger of falling victim to 'bad faith', inauthenticity. And so far as religion is concerned, it has had a direct and significant impact, in particular being seen by certain Lutheran theologians as lending fresh force and impetus to the tradition to which they belong. Thus an emphatic repudiation of reason in favour of non-rational commitment and surrender to divine grace is fundamental to positions expounded in our own period through the voluminous works of men like Emil Brunner and Karl Barth. Reason, according to Brunner, 'is not given us to know God, but to know the world'; and while neither he nor Barth has wished in any way to qualify the transcendent claims of Christianity, they have been at one in denouncing the 'misplaced intellectualism' of trying to apply to them standards appropriate to natural knowledge and rational enquiry. In this, as in many of their other contentions, the Kierkegaardian echoes are clear.

The depth and importance of Kierkegaard's influence within the religious domain must certainly be granted; at the same time, its extent ought not to be exaggerated. If there have been some Christian thinkers who have welcomed his ideas as affording a barrier against the presumptions and incursions of rationalism, there are also those who have protested that they do so at the cost of giving no grounds for preferring Christianity to any other religion or system of belief and even of robbing it of all serious pretensions to credibility. Obviously a good deal depends here on how the ideas in question are taken. It is one thing to regard acceptance of the Christian faith as commitment to a self-contained sphere or 'form of life', not itself finally justifiable by external criteria or modes of assessment; it is another to treat its content as being in some sense essentially paradoxical, avowedly 'absurd' or contradictory. In so far as Kierkegaard subscribed to the second, and not merely to the first, of these positions, his standpoint has been felt – not unnaturally – to present special problems.

Such considerations, however, raise issues with philosophical and theological ramifications that extend far beyond the scope of the present study. Nor should they be allowed to obscure from view those other features of Kierkegaard's work which have attracted later generations and which can only be fully appreciated by reading his own writings: the singular intensity of his vision of human existence, the literary originality and imagination he showed in exploring its various possibilities, and the vivid sense he conveyed of what the struggle to achieve and preserve religious faith can mean to one who was himself acutely conscious of its difficulties. It was perhaps these qualities in particular that appealed to Ludwig Wittgenstein, who expressed a profound respect for him and whose fragmentary but suggestive remarks on the distinctive and autonomous character of religious belief often call him to mind. On one occasion Wittgenstein observed:

> An honest religious thinker is like a tightrope walker. He almost looks as though he were walking on nothing but air. His support is the slenderest imaginable. And yet it really is possible to walk on it.

I do not know whether he was thinking specifically of Kierkegaard when he wrote these words, although it seems very likely. In any case, they may stand.

References

Chapter 2

The quotation from Hegel on p. 30 is taken from the first part of his *Encyclopaedia of the Philosophical Sciences*, tr. W. Wallace as *The Logic of Hegel* (Oxford, 1968), 335.

Chapter 4

'. . . about which we feel most assured' (p. 64–5): for a trenchant critique along these lines, see Brand Blanshard, *Reason and Belief* (London, 1974), 234–40.

Chapter 5

The quotations from Lessing on p. 72 are taken from *Lessing's Theological Writings*, ed. and tr. Henry Chadwick (Stanford, 1956), 54–5, 83.

'. . . belief implicit in the *Fragments*' (p. 81): for illuminating discussions of these connections, see Richard Popkin, 'Hume and Kierkegaard', in the *Journal of Religion*, vol. 31 (1951), 274–81, and Terence Penelhum, *God and Scepticism* (Dordrecht, 1983), chs. 4–6. For an account of Hume's relation to Hamann, see also Isaiah Berlin, 'Hume and the Sources of German Anti-Rationalism', in his *Against the Current: Essays in the History of Ideas* (London, 1979). The quotation from Hume on p. 82 is taken from *Hume's Enquiries* (Oxford, 1936), 131.

'. . . distorted the meaning of Christianity' (p. 89): in his *Essence of Christianity* (1841), which Kierkegaard had read, Feuerbach did not deny that Hegel's interpretation apparently conflicted with some of the cardinal tenets of Christian orthodoxy. Unlike Kierkegaard, though, and in line with the master's own official doctrine, he maintained that this was due to Hegel's having replaced an 'inconsequent' and 'undeveloped' mode of thinking by one that came closer to identifying its true significance.

'. . . traditional forms of validation or support' (p. 104): see Paul Edwards, 'Kierkegaard and the "Truth" of Christianity', in *Philosophy*, vol. 46 (1971), 97–100.

Chapter 7
The quotation from Wittgenstein on p. 121 is taken from *Culture and Value*, tr. Peter Winch (Oxford, 1980), 73.

Further reading

Writings by Kierkegaard

The Danish edition of Kierkegaard's collected works [*Samlede Vaerker*] is edited by A. B. Drachman, J. L. Heiberg, and H. O. Lange (20 vols., Copenhagen, Gyldendal, 1963–4). A scholarly English edition of Kierkegaard's writings, under the general editorship of H. V. Hong, has been published by Princeton University Press (26 vols., 1978–2000). A very useful, single-volume selection from the Princeton edition is *The Essential Kierkegaard*, edited by H. V. and E. H. Hong (2000).

The following is a selection of translated works additional to those referred to in the note on abbreviations:

The Concept of Irony, tr. H. V. and E. H. Hong (Princeton University Press, 1989).

Purity of Heart is to Will One Thing, tr. D. V. Steere (Harper Torchback, 1958).

Training in Christianity, tr. W. Lowrie (Oxford University Press, 1941).

Works of Love, tr. H. V. and E. H. Hong (Harper Torchback, 1962).

Attack upon 'Christendom', tr. W. Lowrie (Princeton University Press, 1944).

The Last Years: Journals 1853–55, tr. R. G. Smith (Harper and Row, 1965).

Writing about Kierkegaard

The best-known biography is W. Lowrie's full and detailed *Kierkegaard* (Oxford University Press, 1938). Josiah Thompson's more astringent and critically penetrating biographical study, *Kierkegaard* (Gollancz, 1974), is excellent and may also be recommended.

The number of available commentaries on various aspects of Kierkegaard's work is vast; there is space to mention only a few. For a good general account, balanced and informative, the reader should consult James Collins's *The Mind of Kierkegaard* (Princeton University Press, 1953; paperback edition, 1983). *Kierkegaard's Authorship* by G. B. and G. E. Arbaugh (Augustana College Library, 1967) includes useful summaries and discussions of all the main published writings, while Louis Mackey's *Kierkegaard: A Kind of Poet* (University of Pennsylvania Press, 1971) provides a perceptive appraisal of its subject from a largely literary point of view. A comprehensive and philosophically orientated analysis of the structure of Kierkegaard's thought is to be found in Alastair Hannay's *Kierkegaard* (Routledge and Kegan Paul, 1982). The historical connections between Hegel and Kierkegaard are explored in scrupulous detail by NielsThulstrup in *Kierkegaard's Relation in Hegel*, tr. G. L. Strengren (Princeton University Press, 1980). Books of more general scope but containing interesting and substantial discussions of Kierkegaard's ideas include the following: *God and Scepticism*, by Terence Penelhum (Reidel Publishing Company, 1983); *Lessing's 'Ugly Ditch': A Study of Theology and History*, by Gordon E. Michalson (Pennsylvania State University Press, 1985); *Reason and Belief*, by Brand Blanshard (Allen and Unwin, 1974); *Existentialism*, by John Macquarrie (Pelican, 1973); and *After Virtue*, by Alasdair MacIntyre (Duckworth, 1981).

Since this book appeared, two useful collections of articles on Kierkegaard have been published: *The Cambridge Companion to Kierkegaard*, edited by A. Hannay and G. Marino (Cambridge University Press, 1998), and *Kierkegaard: A Critical Reader*, edited by J. Reé and

J. Chamberlain. A valuable study of Kierkegaard's moral philosophy is Anthony Rudd, *Kierkegaard and the Limits of the Ethical* (Clarendon Press, 1997). Two interesting discussions of Kierkegaard's philosophical theology are David R. Law, *Kierkegaard as Negative Theologian* (Clarendon Press, 1993) and M. Jamie Ferreira, *Transforming Vision: Imagination and Will in Kierkegaardian Faith* (Clarendon Press, 1991). Kierkegaard's relation to currents of contemporary European philosophy is discussed in Michael Weston, *Kierkegaard and Modern Continental Philosophy* (Routledge, 1994). C. Stephen Evans, *Passionate Reason: Making Sense of Kierkegaard's* Philosophical Fragments (Indiana University Press, 1992) is a rewarding examination, not only of *Philosophical Fragments*, but of Kierkegaard's wider thought. A difficult, but rewarding, reading of several of Kierkegaard's works as 'subversive' texts is included in Stephen Mulhall, *Inheritance and Originality: Wittgenstein, Heidegger, Kierkegaard* (Clarendon Press, 2001).

Index